TEXTS AND TRANSLATIONS 4

EARLY CHRISTIAN LITERATURE SERIES

1

A PSEUDO-EPIPHANIUS

TESTIMONY BOOK

Edited and translated by

Robert V. Hotchkiss

SOCIETY OF BIBLICAL LITERATURE

AND

SCHOLARS' PRESS

1974

A PSEUDO-EPIPHANIUS

TESTIMONY BOOK

Printed in the United States of America
SCHOLARS' PRESS
University of Montana
Missoula, Montana 59801

TEXTS AND TRANSLATIONS is a project of the Committee on Research and Publications of the Society of Biblical Literature, and is under the general direction of George W. MacRae (Harvard University), Executive Secretary of the Society, and Harry M. Orlinsky (Hebrew Union College-Jewish Institute of Religion, New York), Chairman of the Committee. The purpose of the project is to make available in convenient and inexpensive format ancient texts which are not easily accessible but are of importance to scholars and students of "biblical literature" as broadly defined by the Society. Reliable modern English translations will accompany the texts. Occasionally the various series will include documents not published elsewhere. It is not a primary aim of these publications to provide authoritative new critical texts, nor to furnish extensive annotations. The editions are regarded as provisional, and individual volumes may be replaced in the future as better textual evidence becomes available. The following subseries have been established thus far:

PSEUDEPIGRAPHA, edited by Robert A. Kraft (University of Pennsylvania)

GRECO-ROMAN RELIGION, edited by Hans Dieter Betz (School of Theology at Claremont)

EARLY CHRISTIAN LITERATURE, edited by Birger A. Pearson (University of California at Santa Barbara)

The EARLY CHRISTIAN LITERATURE SERIES is intended to include texts from Christian literature through the early patristic period, with the exception of those that belong properly in the PSEUDEPIGRAPHA SERIES. The volumes in this series are selected, prepared, and edited in consultation with the following editorial committee:

Birger A. Pearson (University of California at Santa Barbara), Editor

Stephen Benko (California State University at Fresno)

John Gager (Princeton University)

William R. Schoedel (University of Illinois at Urbana)

Wilhelm Wuellner (Pacific School of Religion)

TABLE OF CONTENTS

PREFACE

This work is representative of what appears to be a relatively
untouched literary sub-genre--the Christian testimony book which is
not overtly anti-Jewish. From available manuscripts, I have prepared
a critical text of a pseudo-Epiphanius Testimony Book, along with a
working translation.

Thanks are due to those who have aided greatly in this enter-
prise, particularly Robert A. Kraft of the University of Pennsylvania,
who has guided the study throughout and provided invaluable assistance;
Marcel Richard of the Institut de recherche et d'histoire des textes
in Paris, who has provided microfilms of texts and much helpful
information; and Robert F. Evans of the University of Pennsylvania,
who has given the text and translation much helpful review and
criticism.

In 1828, vol. 13 of *Memorie di Religione, di Morale e di Letteratura* published the Greek text and a Latin translation of a Testimony Book (=TB), attributed in its title to Epiphanius, Archbishop of Cyprus. This material came from the literary remains of Stefano Antonio Morcelli (1737-1822), librarian of the Albano Library at the Vatican. Morcelli had prepared the text for the printer, and included a preface in which he tried to identify the work. He gave it the title *De divina inhumanatione*, believing it to be another form of a lost work by that title listed in the Syriac catalogue of Epiphanius' works by the 14th century Nestorian Ebedjesu.[1] This lost work was thought by William Cave to have been a treatment of the generation and incarnation of Christ.[2]

The manuscript from which Morcelli was working is presently catalogued as codex Vaticanus Graecus 790. It is a rather small paper MS (14.6 x 10.7 cm) which contains a number of assorted patristic works. The TB is on ff. 134v to 150v, item no. 30. It is immediately preceded by two short works attributed to Athanasius[3] and a short work attributed to Ephraem Syrus,[4] and is followed by an epitome of Epiphanius' *Weights and Measures* attributed in the margin to Cyril of Alexandria.[5] The MS is dated by the Vatican cataloguer to the 14th century,[6] and is written in a clear, legible hand. Comparison of a

---

[1]As reprinted in G. S. Assemani, *Bibliotheca Orientalis Clementino-Vaticana* 3 (Rome, 1725) 1.42-43.

[2]William Cave, *Chartophylax Ecclesiasticus* (London, 1685) 45.

[3]*Questions to the Prince of Antioch, no. 137*, and *Fifth Dialogue on the Holy Trinity*.

[4]*On Strength and Suffering*.

[5]In his edition of the Syriac version of *Weights and Measures* (Chicago, 1935), J. E. Dean mentions only 5 Greek MSS plus some fragments and excerpts, none of which has the title in the first hand. Neither he nor Quasten report a Cyril of Alexandria epitome.

[6]Robert Devreesse (ed.), *Codices Vaticani Graeci* (Rome, 1950) 3.307-311.

2

microfilm of the MS with Morcelli's printed text shows that the latter
is frequently inaccurate in details, although sufficiently adequate to
provide a satisfactory idea of the work.

One other MS of the TB is known--codex Athos Iviron 28, dated by
Lambros to the 13th century, but by Gregory-Aland to the 14th.[7] It is
a bit larger, perhaps 20 x 14 cm, but is much more difficult to read,
being written in light gray ink on gray parchment in a somewhat more
cursive hand.[8] The TB comes third in the codex, on ff. 246r to 253r,
after the "Epistles of the Apostles" and the four gospels, and is
followed by the same epitome of *Weights and Measures* attributed in the
margin to Cyril of Alexandria.

Relations between the preserved manuscripts

The two manuscripts of the Testimony Book, codex Vaticanus Graecus
790 and codex Athos Iviron 28, are quite closely related. The orthog-
raphy and system of abbreviations are similar, but not identical. Each
uses the normal abbreviations: $\overline{\theta\varsigma}$, $\overline{X\varsigma}$, $\overline{oup\varsigma}$, $\overline{\alpha\nu\gamma\varsigma}$, $\overline{\varkappa\varsigma}$, etc. In addi-
tion, MS 28 tends to abbreviate or omit more grammatical endings than
MS 790. In the table of contents, where the titles in MS 28 are made
to fit two or three to a line, the abbreviations sometimes become
quite radical. Both MSS contain a number of itacisms, MS 790 more
than MS 28. The most conspicuous of these is a use of μητά for μετά
consistently in MS 790 and occasionally in MS 28. Both MSS occasionally use ει for η and o for ω. MS 28 follows the practice of spelling
out the Psalm numbers in full, while MS 790 consistently abbreviates
them. These editorial practices were not considered of sufficient
importance to note them in the apparatus.

The most noteworthy peculiarity about MS 28 is in its numbering
of chapters. Perhaps an editor thought that the proper number of

[7]Spyr. P. Lambros, *Catalogue of the Greek Manuscripts on Mt.
Athos* (Cambridge, 1895/1900) 2.4. Information on the Gregory-Aland
dating from Marcel Richard.

[8]I am very grateful to Marcel Richard, recently retired from the
Institut de recherche et d'histoire des textes in Paris, for informing
me of the existence of this MS, and for being so kind as to photograph
it and provide a microfilm. Prof. Kurt Aland of the Institut für Neu-
testamentliche Textforschung at Münster also kindly made his photo-
graphs of the MS available.

chapters should be 100, even when there really were 102, or perhaps
two additional chapters were inserted in the work after the numbering
was set. In MS 28, there are two chapters numbered 43, so that the
chapter numbers then run one behind MS 790 from 44 to 95, where MS 28
omits the number entirely, to pick up at chapter 96 by calling it
chapter 94. An editor of MS 28 would have had an excellent opportunity
to alter the numbering at chapter 23, which is entirely missing in that
MS. Instead, the next chapter is numbered 24 in both MSS.

The table of contents which heads the TB in both MSS does not
appear to have been carefully correlated with the text. There are at
least ten section rubrics in the table of contents which do not per-
fectly reflect the body of the work itself.[9] Also, in MS 28, the
method of getting the number of chapters to come out to 100 is different in the table of contents from that in the body. Although there
may be two number 43's, as in the body,[10] there are also two number
90's, so that the enumeration still comes out two less than the actual
count.

The close relationship of the two MSS is evidenced by a number of
factors:

In TB 5.10, MS 28 has the form δῆλων, while MS 790 has the more
proper form δῆλον. However, written above the second vowel in MS 790
is a tiny omega, perhaps indicating that this form was found in the
text being copied or in a text with which it was compared, and the
copyist was not quite sure which was correct.

In TB 87.1, the form ἀνταποδώσεως is written with a rather unusual abbreviation for the grammatical ending. This abbreviation is
found at this place in both MSS, but not in other instances of the
same grammatical form.

In TB 88.4, MS 28 reproduces two lines of Ps 18.5, while MS 790
contains only the first line and a short statement: "and the rest."
Either the copyist of MS 790 felt that the next line was too well
known to bother with, or else the copyist of MS 28 felt that an "etc."

---

[9] See section rubrics 41, 59, 63, 64, 69, 70, 71, 79, 85, 91.
Rubrics 70 and 71 are also reversed in the table of contents from
their order in the main body of the text.

[10] The MS is extremely difficult to read at this point, and the
numbers in the left margin have been lost by being stitched into the
binding.

was unworthy of such a work and supplied the line which the other omitted.

There are three examples of homoioteluton in MS 790, in which the copyist jumped from a word in one line of his source to a similar word in the next line. These are found in TB 49.1-2, 58.1, and perhaps 88.4. There are no examples of this error in MS 28, although in TB 43.1, for no obvious reason, MS 28 lacks a whole poetic line of Ps 40 which MS 790 contains. Most of the "omissions" in MS 28, in contrast to MS 790, concern single words, often in introductory material, and usually of relatively little consequence to the meaning of the passage. That these "omissions" are supplied in MS 790 would seem to indicate either that the latter copyist had a better vorlage, or that the passages being cited were so familiar that the missing words could be supplied from memory.

In TB 89.2 and 89.3, MS 28 inverts the usual word order for the introductory formula for a quotation from the Psalms, while MS 790 wholly omits the word ψαλμῷ. This could indicate either that MS 28 supplied a word at the end of the phrase which MS 790 omits, or that MS 790 dropped the word because it seemed out of place in the different word order.

In the section rubric for TB 66, MS 28 has an extremely unusual abbreviation or letter at the end of the word τύπον while MS 790 has the rather odd form τυπονι. Again, either could be a correction of the other, or an attempt to rectify an unusual form.

In TB 77, both MSS omit the last two letters of μαρτύριον in the section rubric. In MS 28, however, the missing letters are supplied by squeezing them in between the lines of the text. This could indicate that MS 28 was copying from a deficient text (MS 790?) and put in the correction as an afterthought, or that MS 790 copied the text as it was in his vorlage (MS 28?) and someone later supplied the missing letters in MS 28, or that both MSS derive from the same deficient textual stream.

In TB 94.2b, MS 790 has παιδίον instead of πεδίον. In MS 28, this page has been "touched up," and is quite easily read, except for that one word, which is smudged. It is possible that the copyist of MS 790 could not read that smudge, and inserted a form which he thought would contain the right number of letters for the amount of space involved. The variant could also be explained as an itacism, but not one which recurs throughout the MSS.

The copyists of MS 28 and MS 790 were both aware of the existence of a chapter 23. The former omitted the chapter, but also skipped the number, while the latter put a note in the lower margin indicating that it was identical to chapter 18. Since it was the copyist of MS 790 who has properly numbered the chapters, it would not seem unlikely that he noticed the omission in his source and supplied a note to indicate what he thought probably went there.

Although one cannot speak with certainty, the evidence, particularly the homoioteluton, seems to lean slightly toward the conclusion that MS 28 is, or witnesses to, the earlier copy, and that MS 790 was copied either from MS 28 or from another copy virtually identical to it in many respects. It is most unlikely that MS 790 could have been an immediate predecessor of MS 28, since the numbering in MS 28 is so strange.

Provenance and purpose

An extended study of the TB[11] has led me to some rather tentative conclusions about the origins of the work. A number of internal factors indicate the possibility that the work existed in essentially the present form by the fourth century or slightly later. The association with Epiphanius, for which the evidence is ambiguous, might give a strong clue as to the date of the work and its provenance. Likewise, several unusual applications of the Jewish scriptures appear to concur with the practices in Asia Minor at the same time.

It is not unlikely that the TB stems from a document which was used in preparation for, or explanation of, the baptism of Christians. The few editorial comments seem to bear on baptism, and chapters 90-92 could reflect the administration of the sacrament itself. This concentration on baptism could explain the lack of reference to any other sacrament, including what seems to be a deliberate avoidance of mention of the Eucharist.

---

[11]Presented as a thesis to the faculty of the Graduate School of the University of Pennsylvania, 1973.

TEXT AND TRANSLATION

The text as printed combines what seem to be the "best" readings of both manuscripts, with a few minor emendations as to spelling and grammar made only when it seemed absolutely necessary. The spelling, versification, and where possible, the punctuation have followed the Göttingen edition of the Jewish Greek scriptures. The notes refer to the two available manuscripts:

28: Codex Athos Iviron 28.

790: Codex Vaticanus Graecus 790.

Τοῦ ἁγίου καὶ μακαρίου
'ΕΠΙΦΑΝΙΟΥ
'Απχιεπισκόπου Κωνσταντίας τῆς Κύπρου
ΜΑΡΤΥΡΙΑΙ
τῶν θεοπνεύστων γραφῶν καὶ ἁγίων
περὶ τῆς ἐξ οὐρανοῦ ἐπὶ τῆς γῆς
τοῦ μονογενοῦς θεοῦ Λόγου παρουσίας,
καὶ τῶν δι' αὐτοῦ γενομένων θαυμάτων
καὶ τοῦ πάθους καὶ τῆς ἀναστάσεως
καὶ τῆς δευτέρας αὐτοῦ καὶ μελλούσης ἐπιφανείας .

ᾱ   ὅτι πρὸ τῶν αἰώνων ὁ υἱὸς γεγένηται--
β̄   ὅτι συνῆν τῷ πατρί--
γ̄   ὅτι συνκτίστης--
δ̄   ὅτι ἀπεστάλη--
ε̄   ὅτι ἥξει--
ϛ̄   ὅτι ὤφθη· καὶ θεὸς ὤν, γέγονεν ἄνθρωπος--
ζ̄   ὅτι ἐκ σπέρματος Δαυιδ ὁ Κύριος--
η̄   ὅτι ἐκ παρθένου--
θ̄   ὅτι μετὰ τὸ γεννηθῆναι φυλάξει τὴν τέκουσαν παρθένον--
ῑ   ὅτι ἡ μήτρα πύλη--
ιᾱ   ὅτι ἀνωδύνος ἡ παρθένος γεννήσει--
ιβ̄   ὅτι ἐχρήσθη--
ιγ̄   ὅτι χωρὶς πατρὸς ἐπὶ γῆς καὶ μιξέως--
ιδ̄   ὅτι παιδίον--
ιε̄   ὅτι ἐν Βηθλεὲμ τεχθήσεται--
ιϛ̄   ὅτι προσκυνήσουσιν οἱ μάγοι--
ιζ̄   ὅτι ἀνατελεῖ ὁ ἀστήρ--
ιη̄   ὅτι τὰ βρέφη ἀναιρεθήσονται--
ιθ̄   ὅτι ταραχθήσεται 'Ηρῴδης καὶ οἱ μετ' αὐτοῦ πάντες--
κ̄   ὅτι ὑποκρίσει ζητήσει προσκυνῆσαι--
κᾱ   ὅτι θυμωθήσεται ἀπατηθείς--
κβ̄   ὅτι ἐρευνήσει καὶ ἀναξητήσει--

Title και αγιων] om 28./ γης om 28.
ᾱ   των] om 28./γεγενηται] γενναται 790.
ιᾱ   ανωδυνος] ανωδινος 28.

By the holy and blessed
EPIPHANIUS
Archbishop of Constantia in Cyprus
TESTIMONIES
of the divinely inspired and holy scriptures
concerning the coming from heaven to earth
of the only Word of God
and the miracles wrought through him
and his passion and resurrection
and his second and future appearing.

1   That before the ages the Son was begotten--

2   That he was with the Father--

3   That he was the joint creator--

4   That he was sent out--

5   That he would come--

6   That he became visible, and being God, became man--

7   That the Lord is from the seed of David--

8   That [he was born] from a virgin--

9   That after his birth, he will protect the virgin who bore him--

10   That the womb is a gate--

11   That the virgin gave birth without travail--

12   That he was annointed--

13   That without a father on earth or intercourse [he was born]--

14   That he was a child--

15   That he would be born in Bethlehem--

16   That the magi would worship him--

17   That the star would rise--

18   That the infants would be slaughtered--

19   That Herod would be disturbed, and all those with him--

20   That with hypocrisy, [Herod] would seek to worship him--

21   That when [Herod] was deceived he would become angry--

22   That Herod would search and look [for him]--

κγ   ὅτι ἀνελεῖ τὰ βρέφη--

κδ   ὅτι οὐκ ἀναλεῖ τὸν Χριστόν--

κε   ὅτι εἰς Αἴγυπτον καταβήσεται ὁ Χριστός--

κϛ   ὅτι ἐξ Αἰγύπτου κληθήσεται--

κζ   ὅτι βαπτιζόμενος ἁγιάσει τὰ ὕδατα--

κη   ὅτι ἐνδόξως ἀπὸ τοῦ βαπτίσματος ἀναβήσεται--

κθ   ὅτι ἐπὶ θαλάσσης περιπατήσει--

λ   ὅτι τὸ κράσπεδον τοῦ ἱματίου αὐτοῦ θεραπεύσει--

λα   ὅτι ξηρανεῖ τὴν συκήν--

λβ   ὅτι πειρασθήσεται ὑπὸ τοῦ διαβόλου--

λγ   ὅτι θεραπεύσει πολλούς--

λδ   ὅτι ἀναστήσει νεκρούς--

λε   ὅτι ἀπιστήσουσιν οἱ Ἰουδαῖοι--

λϛ   ὅτι ἀπὸ πέντε ἄρτων θρέψει πολλούς--

λζ   ὅτι ἐπὶ ὄνου εἰς τήν Σιων ἐπελεύσεται--

λη   ὅτι τὰ βρέφη προδράμουσι κράζοντα τὸ εὐλογήμενος ὁ ἐρχόμενος--

λθ   ὅτι ἐλέγξει τὸν λαόν--

μ   ὅτι ἐπιχυθήσεται αὐτῷ νάρδος--

μα   ὅτι συναχθήσονται κατ' αὐτοῦ--

μβ   ὅτι καταψευδομαρτυρήσουσιν--

μγ   ὅτι Ιουδας προδώσει--

μδ   ὅτι ἐρεῖ ὁ Ιουδας Χαῖρε ῥαββί--

με   ὅτι ἀργυρίου πραθήσεται--

μϛ   ὅτι δήσουσι τὸν Χριστόν--

μζ   ὅτι κρίνουσιν αὐτόν--

μη   ὅτι ῥαπίσουσιν αὐτον καὶ ἐξουθενήσουσι--

μθ   ὅτι φεύξονται οἱ ἀπόστολοι--

ν   ὅτι ἀρνήσεται Πέτρος--

να   ὅτι σταυρώσουσιν αὐτόν--

νβ   ὅτι ἀκάνθαις στεφανώσουσιν αὐτόν--

νγ   ὅτι ὄξος καὶ χολὴν ποτίσουσιν αὐτόν--

νδ   ὅτι κόκκινον ἱμάτιον ἐνδύσουσιν αὐτόν--

μβ καταψευδομαρτυρησουσιν] ψευδομαρτυρησουσιν 790.
μγ προδωσει] προδοσει 28, 790.
μη ραπισουσιν] ρηπησουσιν 28, 790. / εξουθενησουσι] εξουθενησωσι 790.
να αυτον] om 28.
νγ ποτισουσιν] ποτησουσιν 28, 790.

23   That [Herod] would annihilate the infants--

24   That [Herod] would not destroy the Christ--

25   That the Christ would go down into Egypt--

26   That he would be called out of Egypt--

27   That when he is baptized, he would sanctify the waters--

28   That he would ascend from his baptism gloriously--

29   That he would walk on the sea--

30   That the hem of his garment would heal--

31   That he would wither the fig tree--

32   That he would be tempted by the devil--

33   That he would heal many--

34   That he would raise the dead--

35   That the Jews would be disbelieving--

36   That from five loaves [of bread] he would feed many--

37   That on an ass he would come into Zion--

38   That the infants would run ahead, crying out, "Blessed is he

39   That he would reprove the people--   [who comes"--

40   That oil of nard would be poured over him--

41   That they would come together against him--

42   That they would bear false witness against him--

43   That Judas would betray [him]--

44   That Judas would say, "Hail, Rabbi"--

45   That he would be sold for silver--

46   That they would bind the Christ--

47   That they would judge him--

48   That they would strike him and despise him--

49   That the apostles would flee--

50   That Peter would deny him--

51   That they would crucify him--

52   That they would crown him with thorns--

53   That they would give him vinegar and gall to drink--

54   That they would put a scarlet robe on him--

$\overline{νε}$ ὅτι σιωπήσει κρινόμενος--

$\overline{νς}$ ὅτι χλευασθήσεται--

$\overline{νζ}$ ὅτι αὐτός ἐστιν ἡ ζωὴ ὁ κρεμμάμενος ἐπὶ ξύλου--

$\overline{νη}$ ὅτι ἀπάθεια τὸ πάθος αὐτοῦ--

$\overline{νθ}$ ὅτι ἐν νυκτί, ψύχους ὄντος καὶ ἀνθρακιᾶς κειμένης πάθη--

$\overline{ξ}$ ὅτι δύσεται ὁ ἥλιος--

$\overline{ξα}$ ὅτι δύσεται ὁ ἥλιος μεσημβρίας--

$\overline{ξβ}$ ὅτι τὰ ἱμάτια αὐτοῦ διαμεριυόνται--

$\overline{ξγ}$ ὅτι συνσταυρωθήσεται λησταῖς--

$\overline{ξδ}$ ὅτι τὴν πλευρὰν ἐκκεντήσουσιν--

$\overline{ξε}$ ὅτι ὀστοῦν αὐτοῦ οὐ συντριβήσεται--

$\overline{ξς}$ ὅτι ἐκ τῆς πλευρᾶς αὐτοῦ ὕδωρ ῥυήσεται εἰς βαπτίσματος τύπον--

$\overline{ξζ}$ ὅτι ἐν πέτρᾳ τεθήσεται--

$\overline{ξη}$ ὅτι λίθος ἡ θύρα τοῦ μνήματος--

$\overline{ξθ}$ ὅτι σφραγίσουσιν αὐτόν--

$\overline{ο}$ ὅτι ταφήσεται--

$\overline{οα}$ ὅτι θέρους ἀρχομένου ἔσται τὸ πάθος, μηνὶ τῷ καθ' ἡμᾶς Μαρτίῳ--

$\overline{οβ}$ ὅτι φοβήσει τὸν Ἅδην ταφείς--

$\overline{ογ}$ ὅτι ἀναμάρτητος--

$\overline{οδ}$ ὅτι ἀναστήσεται--

$\overline{οε}$ ὅτι μάτην οἱ στρατιῶται τὸν τάφον τηρήσουσιν--

$\overline{ος}$ ὅτι πρωὶ ἡ ἀνάστασις--

$\overline{οζ}$ ὅτι μαρτύριον ὁ τόπος ἔσται--

$\overline{οη}$ ὅτι ἀπὸ τοῦ προτειχίσματος--

$\overline{οθ}$ ὅτι ζητηθήσεται ὑπὸ τῶν γυναικῶν--

$\overline{π}$ ὅτι πρῶτον ἀπαντήσει γυναιξί--

$\overline{πα}$ ὅτι ἀναχωρήσουσιν ἔμφοβοι--

$\overline{πβ}$ ὅτι ἐμφυσήσει τοῖς ἀποστόλοις τὸ πνεῦμα τὸ ἅγιον--

$\overline{πγ}$ ὅτι ἀπὸ μέλιτος κηρίου φάγεται μετὰ τὴν ἀνάστασιν--

$\overline{πδ}$ ὅτι ἐροῦσιν ὅτι ἐκλάπη--

$\overline{πε}$ ὅτι οἱ νεκροὶ ἀναστήσονται--

$\overline{πς}$ ὅτι εἰς οὐρανοὺς ἀναλεύσεται--

$\overline{νζ}$ κρεμμαμενος] κρεμαμενος 790.
$\overline{ξς}$ εις...τυπον] τυπον βαπτισματος 790.
$\overline{οβ}$ ταφεις] ταφης 28, 790.
$\overline{οθ}$ των] om 28.
$\overline{π}$ γυναιξι] γυναικας 28, γυναιοιος 790.

55   That he would be silent while being judged--

56   That he would be mocked--

57   That he is the life which hangs on the wooden stake--

58   That his passion would be passionless--

59   That in the night, when it was cold and there was a charcoal
      fire, he would suffer--

60   That the sun would set--

61   That the sun would set at midday--

62   That his garments would be divided--

63   That he would be crucified with insurgents--

64   That they would pierce [his] side--

65   That a bone of his would not be broken--

66   That from his side water would flow (as a type indicating

67   That he would be placed in a rock--   [baptizing)--

68   That the door of the tomb would be a stone--

69   That they would seal it--

70   That he would be buried--

71   That the suffering would be at the beginning of summer, in the
      month which we call March--

72   That his being buried would terrify Hades--

73   That he would be without sin--

74   That he would be raised up--

75   That the soldiers would guard the tomb in vain--

76   That the resurrection would be in the early morning--

77   That the place would be a witness--

78   That [the resurrection would be] from inside the wall--

79   That he would be sought by the women--

80   That he would meet women first--

81   That they would run away terrified--

82   That he would breathe the Holy Spirit into the apostles--

83   That after the resurrection he would eat from honey of the
      honeycomb--

84   That they would say that [his body] was stolen--

85   That the dead would be raised up--

86   That he would be taken up into heaven--

π͞ζ   ὅτι αὐτὸς ἦν ὁ κηρύξας--

π͞η   ὅτι ἐν πάσῃ τῇ γῇ τὸ ὄνομα αὐτοῦ--

π͞θ   ὅτι ἐκ δεξιῶν τοῦ πατρός, οὐκ ἀφ' οὗ ἀνῆλθεν ἐκάθισε· ἀλλὰ καὶ

ϙ͞   ὅτι κληθησόμεθα Χριστιανοί--   [πρὸ τούτου--

ϙ͞α   ὅτι καὶ ἡ μετώπου σημείσωσις τοῦ σταυροῦ προκατηγγέλετο--

ϙ͞β   ὅτι τὸ ἐν Χριστῷ βάπτισμα προκατηγγέλλετο--

ϙ͞γ   ὅτι προκατηγγέλλετο ἡ δευτέρα παρουσία--

ϙ͞δ   ὅτι κρινεῖ τὴν οἰκουμένην καὶ αὐτῷ ἡ κρίσις δοθήσεται--

ϙ͞ε   ὅτι ὁ ἥλιος καὶ ἡ σελήνη σκοτισθήσονται--

ϙ͞ϛ   ὅτι οἱ οὐρανοὶ εἰλίσονται--

ϙ͞ζ   ὅτι πρὸ τῆς Χριστοῦ παρουσίας ἥξει ὁ Ἀντίχριστος--

ϙ͞η   ὅτι φονεύσει πολλούς--

ϙ͞θ   ὅτι τότε καιρὸς θλίψεως--

ρ͞   ὅτι καὶ μετ' αὐτὸν καὶ πῶς ὁ Χριστός--

ρ͞α   ὅτι τὸ σημεῖον τοῦ Χριστοῦ φανερὸν ἔσται--

ρ͞β   ὅτι τῆς βασιλείας οὐκ ἕξει πέρας--

[1]   α͞ ὅτι πρὸ αἰώνων ὁ υἱὸς γεγέννηται--

   [.1]   Δαυιδ ὁ μέγας πρῶτος λέγει ἐν τῷ ρ͞θ ψαλμῷ·
               Ἐκ γαστρὸς πρὸ ἑωσφόρου ἐγέννηισά σε.

   [.2]   Καὶ ἡ Σοφια δὲ ὁμοίως λέγει·
               Πρὸ τοῦ αἰῶνος ἐθεμελίωσέ με ἐν ἀρχῇ,
               πρὸ τοῦ τὴν γῆν ποιῆσαι
               καὶ πρὸ τοῦ τὰς ἀβύσσους,
               καὶ πρὸ τοῦ προελθεῖν τὰς πηγὰς των ὑδάτων,
               καὶ πρὸ τοῦ ὄρη ἑδρασθῆναι,
               πρὸ δὲ πάντων βουνῶν γεννᾷ με.

   [.3]   Καὶ Δαυιδ αὖθις λέγει ἐν ο͞α ψαλμῷ·
               Συμπαραμενεῖ τῷ ἡλίῳ
               καὶ πρὸ τῆς σελήνης γενεὰς γενεῶν.

ρ͞   και] om 28.
ρ͞β   ουκ] αυτου γη 790.
1.3 αυθις...ψαλμω] εν ο͞α ψαλμω λεγει 28.
     γενεας γενεων] γεννεας γεννεων 28.

87   That he was the herald--

88   That his name [would be known] in the whole earth--

89   That he sat at the right hand of the father, not only after he
     ascended, but even before that--

90   That we would be called Christians--

91   That even the mark of the cross on the forehead was foretold--

92   That baptism in Christ was foretold--

93   That the second coming was foretold--

94   That he would judge the inhabited world, and the judgment would
     be given to him--

95   That the sun and moon would be darkened--

96   That the heavens would be rolled up--

97   That before the appearing of Christ the Antichrist would come--

98   That he would kill many--

99   That the time of tribulation would come--

100 That somehow the Christ also would come with him--

101 That the sign of Christ would be plainly seen--

102 That the kingdom would not have an end--

1 That before the ages the Son was begotten--

.1   David, the mighty one, first says in the 109th Psalm,
        From the womb I begat you before the morning star.   [Ps 109.3]

.2   And Wisdom similarly says,

        Before this age he established me, in the beginning,
        before the creation of the earth
        and before the creation of the depths,
        and before the fountains of waters came forth,
        and before the mountains were made,
        before all hills he begets me.   [Prov 8.23-25]

.3   And in the 71st Psalm, David says again,

        He will endure as long as the sun
        and before the moon to all generations.   [Ps 71.5]

2-4.4

[2]   β̄ ὅτι συνῆν τῷ πατρί--

      Μωυσης λέγει ἐν τῇ κτίσει τοῦ κόσμου·

      Ποιήσωμεν ἄνθροπον κατ' εἰκόνα ἡμετέραν καὶ
      καθ' ὁμοίωσιν.

[3]   γ̄ ὅτι συνκτίστης--

   [.1]   Ἡ Σοφια λέγει·

      Ἡνίκα ἡτοίμαζε τὸν οὐρανόν, συμπαρήμην αὐτῷ·
      καὶ ὅτε ἀφώριζε τὸν ἑαυτοῦ θρόνον·
      καὶ ἡνίκα ἐπ' ἀνέμων ἰσχυρὰ ἐποίει τὰ ἄνω νέφη·
      καὶ ὡς ἀσφαλεῖς ἐτίθει πηγὰς τὰς ὑπ' οὐρανόν·
      καὶ ἡνίκα ἰσχυρὰ ἐποίει τὰ θεμέλια τῆς γῆς,
      ἤμην παρ' αὐτῷ ἁρμόζουσα.

   [.2]   Καὶ Δαυιδ ἐν τῷ λ̄β̄ ψαλμῷ λέγει·

      Τῷ λόγῳ Κυρίου οἱ οὐρανοὶ ἐστερεώθησαν,
      καὶ τῷ πνεύματι τοῦ στόματος αὐτοῦ πᾶσα ἡ δύναμις
      αυτῶν.

   [.3]   Καὶ πάλιν ἡ Σοφια λέγει·

      Εἶδα τὰ ἔργα σου παροῦσα,
      ὅτε ἐποίεις τὸν κόσμον.

[4]   δ̄ ὅτι ἀπεστάλη--

   [.1]   Ησαϊας οὕτως λέγει·

      Κύριος ὁ θεὸς ὁ ποιήσας τὸν οὐρανόν, καὶ πήξας
      αὐτόν, ὁ στερεώσας τὴν γῆν καὶ τὰ ἐν αὐτῇ, καὶ
      διδοὺς πνοὴν τῷ λαῷ τῷ ἐπ' αὐτῆς, καὶ πνοήν τοῖς
      πατοῦσιν αὐτήν· ἐγὼ Κύριος ὁ θεὸς ὁ κάλεσάς σε,
      καὶ ἔδωκά σε εἰς διαθήκην γένους, εἰς φῶς ἐθνῶν,
      ἀνοῖξαι ὀφθαλμοὺς τυφλῶν, ἐξαγαγεῖν ἐκ δεσμῶν
      δεδεμένους, καὶ ἐξ οἴκου φυλῆς, καθημένους ἐν
      σκότει.

   [.2]   Καὶ Μαλαχιας λέγει·

      Ἰδοὺ ἐγὼ ἀποστέλλω τὸν ἄγγελόν μου πρὸ προσώπου
      σου, καὶ ἐπιβλέψεται ὁδόν.

   [.3]   Καὶ πάλιν·

      Εὐαγγελίσασθαι πτωχοῖς ἀπέσταλκέ με.

   [.4]   Καὶ Δαυιδ ἐν τῷ ρ̄ς̄ ψαλμῷ λέγει·

      Ἀπέστειλε τὸν λόγον αὐτοῦ καὶ ἰάσατο αὐτούς.

---

2   Μωυσης] Μωησης 790.
3.2   αυτων] αυτου 790.
3.3   λεγει] om 28. / εργα] εργα και 28.
4   απεσταλη] απεσταλης 28.
4.1   ουτως] om 790. / τω λαω] των λαω 28.

2 That he was with the Father--

Moses says in the [passage on the] creation of the world--
Let us make man according to our image and likeness. [Gen 1.26]

3 That he was the joint-creator--

.1 Wisdom says,

When he prepared the heaven, I was present with him,
and when he set the bounds of his throne,
and when upon the winds he strengthened the upper clouds,
and when he securely founded the fountains under heaven,
and when he strengthened the foundations of the earth,
I was beside him fitting [them all] together.   [Prov 8.27-30]

.2 And in the 32d Psalm, David says,

By the word of the Lord the heavens were established,
and by the breath of his mouth all their power.   [Ps 32.6]

.3 And again Wisdom says,

Since I was present, I saw your works
when you made the world.   [Wis 9.9]

4 That he was sent out--

.1 Isaiah says as follows,

The Lord God, who made the heaven and built it, who established the earth and the things in it, and gives breath to
the people on it, even breath to those who tread on it: I
am the Lord God who called you, and I established you as a
covenant race, for a light to the nations to open the eyes
of the blind, to lead from prison those who are bound, and
those who sit in darkness from the prison-house.   [Isa 42.5-7]

.2 And Malachi says,

Behold, I am sending my messenger before your face, and he
will keep his mind fixed on the way.   [Mal 3.1]

.3 And again,

He sent me to preach good tidings to the poor.   [Isa 61:1]

.4 And in the 106th Psalm, David says,

He sent his word and healed them.   [Ps 106:20]

5-5.12

[5]   ε̄ ὅτι ἥξει--

   [.1]   Ιακωβ λέγει·

       Οὐκ ἐκλείψει ἄρχων ἐκ Ιουδα
       καὶ ἡγούμενος ἐκ τῶν μηρῶν αὐτοῦ,
       ἕως οὗ ἔλξῃ ὃ ἀπόκειται,
       καὶ αὐτὸς προσδοκίαν ἐθνῶν.

   [.2]   Μωυσης λέγει·

       Προφήτην ὑμῖν ἀναστήσει Κύριος ὁ θεὸς ἐκ τῶν
       ἀδελφῶν αὐτοῦ ὡς ἐμε· αὐτοῦ ἀκούσεσθε κατὰ πάντα·
       καὶ ἔσται ὃς ἂν μὴ ἀκούσῃ τοῦ προφήτου ἐκείνου,
       ἐξολοθρευθήσεται εἰς τὸν αἰῶνα.

   [.3]   Καὶ Ωσηε λέγει·

       'ως ὄρθρον ἕτοιμον εὑρήσομεν αὐτόν· καὶ ἥξει ὡς
       ὑετὸς πρώϊμος καὶ ὄψιμος τῇ γῇ.

   [.4]   Καὶ Αμμως λέγει·

       Ἐν τῇ ἡμέρα ἐκείνῃ ἀναστήσει τήν σκηνὴν Δαυιδ
       τὴν πεπτωκυῖαν, καὶ ἀνοικοδομήσει τὰ πεπρωκότα
       αὐτῆς.

   [.5]   Μιχαιας λέγει·

       Ἐπὶ τὰς κορυφὰς τῶν ὀρέων, ἐκ Σιων ἐξελεύσεται
       νόμος, καὶ λόγος Κυρίου ἐξ Ιερουσαλημ.

   [.6]   Καὶ Ιωηλ λέγει·

       Κύριος ἐκ Σιων ἀνακεκράξεται, καὶ ἐξ Ιερουσαλημ
       δώσει φωνὴν αὐτοῦ.

   [.7]   Καὶ πάλιν·

       Γνώσεσθε ὅτι Κύριος ὁ θεὸς ἡμῶν, καὶ κατασκηνώσει
       ἐν ὤρει ἁγίῳ αὐτοῦ.

   [.8]   Καὶ πάλιν·

       Κύριος κατασκηνώσει ἐν Σιων.

   [.9]   Αβδιου λέγει·

       Ἐν τῷ ὄρει Σιων ἔσται σωτηρία· ἐγγυς γὰρ ἡμέρδ
       Κυρίου ἐπὶ πάντα τὰ ἔθνη.

   [.10]   Ὁ δὲ Ιωνας ἀρκέσει τὸν τύπον τοῦ θανάτου δῆλον.

   [.11]   Καὶ Ναουμ λέγει·

     [a.]   Χρηστὸς ὁ Κύριος τοῖς ὑπομένουσιν αὐτόν.

     [b.]   Ἰδοὺ γὰρ ἐγὼ ἐπὶ σέ, λέγει Κύριος παντοκράτωρ.

   [.12]   Καὶ Αβακουμ·

5.2 ακουσεσθε...παντα] ακουσεσθαι παντες 790.
5.4 ανοικοδομησει] ανοικοδομησω 28.
5.10 δηλον] δηλων 28, 790 mg.

5 That he would come--

.1 Jacob says,

A ruler will not fail from Judah,
nor a prince from his loins
until he comes who is destined,
and he is the expectation of nations.   [Gen 49:10]

.2 Moses says,

The Lord God will raise up a prophet for you from his
brothers, like me; listen to him in all things. And it will
be that whoever does not listen to that prophet will be
utterly destroyed forever.   [Deut 18:15-19]

.3 And Hosea says,

We will find him ready as the morning; and he will come to
the earth as the early and late rain.   [Hos 6:3]

.4 And Amos says,

In that day he will raise up the tabernacle of David that has
fallen, and he will rebuild its ruins.   [Amos 9:11]

.5 Micah says,

On the tops of the mountains, out of Zion will go forth a law,
and the word of the Lord from Jerusalem.   [Mic 4:1-2]

.6 And Joel says,

The Lord will shout from Zion, and will send his voice from
Jerusalem.   [Joel 4:16]

.7 And again,

You will know that the Lord is our God, and he will dwell in
his holy mountain.   [Joel 4:17]

.8 And again,

The Lord will dwell in Zion.   [Joel 4:21]

.9 Obadiah says,

There will be salvation on Mount Zion; for the day of the Lord
is near upon all the nations.   [Obad 15,17]

.10 And Jonah clearly suffices as a type of [his] death.

.11 And Nahum says,

a. The Lord is good to those who wait for him,   [Nah 1:7]

b. for behold, I am over you, says the Lord almighty.   [Nah 2:14]

.12 And Habbakuk,

5.12-5.21

'Ανατελεῖ εἰς πέρας καὶ εἰς καιρόν· καὶ ἐὰν
ὑστερήσει ὑπόμεινον αὐτόν, ὅτι ἐρχόμενος ἥξει
καὶ οὐ χρονίσῃ.

[.13]   Καὶ πάλιν·

'Εν τῷ παρεῖναι τὸν καιρὸν ἀναδειχθήσει.

[.14]   Καὶ ὅτι

'Ο Θεὸς ἀπὸ θαιμαν ἥξει.

[.15]   Καὶ Σοφονιας λέγει·

Χαῖρε σφόδρα, θύγατερ Σιων, κήρυσσε θύγατερ
Ιερουσαλημ· εὐφραίνου καὶ κατ' τέρπου ἐξ ὅλης
τῆς καρδίας σου· περιεῖλε Κύριος τὰ ἀδικήματα σου·
λελύτρωταί σε ἐκ χειρὸς ἐχθρῶν σου. Βασιλεύσει
Κύριος ἐν μέσῳ σου, οὐκ ὄψῃ κακὰ οὐκετι.

[.16]   Καὶ πάλιν·

Θάρσει Σιων, μὴ παρείσθωσαν αἱ χεῖρές σου· Κύριος
ὁ Θεὸς ἐν σοί, δυνατὸς σῶσαι σε.

[.17]   Καὶ Αγγαιος λέγει·

'Εγώ εἰμι μεθ' ὑμῶν, λέγει Κύριος, καὶ τὸ πνεῦμά μου
ἐφέστηκεν ἐφ' ὑμᾶς.

[.18]   Καὶ Ζαχαριας λέγει·

Χαῖρε σφόδρα, θύγατερ Σιων, ὅτι ἰδοὺ ἐγὼ ἔρχομαι,
καὶ κατασκηνώσω ἐν μέσῳ σου, λέγει Κύριος.

[.19]   Καὶ πάλιν·

'Ιδοὺ ἀνήρ, ἀνατολὴ ὄνομα αὐτῷ, καὶ ὑποκάτωθεν
αὐτοῦ ἀνατελεῖ.

[.20]   Καὶ πάλιν·

Τάδε λέγει Κύριος παντοκράτωρ, ἐπιστρέψω ἐπὶ
Σιων, καὶ κατασκηνώσω ἐν μέσῳ Ιερουσαλημ, καὶ
κληθήσεται Ιερουσαλημ πόλις ἀληθινή.

[.21]   Καὶ Μαλαχιας λέγει·

[a.]   Βασιλεὺς μέγας ἐγώ εἰμι, λέγει Κύριος παντοκράτωρ, καὶ τὸ ὄνομά μου ἐπιφανὲς ἔσται ἐν τοῖς
ἔθνεσι.

[b.]   Καὶ ἐξαίφνης ἥξει εἰς τὸν ναὸν αὐτοῦ, λέγει Κύριος
ὁ θεός, ὃν ὑμεῖς θέλετε, καὶ ὁ ἄγγελος τῆς
διαθήκης, ὃν ὑμεῖς ζητεῖτε· ἰδοὺ ἔρχεται, λέγει
Κύριος.

5.14 θαιμαν] θεμαν 790.
5.15 κήρυσσε] κηρυστε 28, κηρυττε 790.
5.16 χειρες] χειραις 790.

He will spring up at the end and at the time; and if he
comes late, wait for him, for the one who comes will come
and will not delay. [Hab 2:3]

.13 And again,

He will be manifested when the time comes. [Hab 3:2]

.14 And that

God will come from Theman. [Hab 3:3]

.15 And Zephaniah says,

Rejoice greatly, daughter of Zion; cry aloud, daughter of
Jerusalem. Rejoice and delight yourself with all your
heart. The Lord has taken away your unrighteousness; he
has ransomed you from the hand of your enemies. The Lord
reigns in your midst; you shall not see evil any
longer. [Zeph 3:14-15]

.16 And again,

Have courage, Zion. Do not let your hands be slack. The
Lord God is in you, able to save you. [Zeph 3:16-17]

.17 And Haggai says,

I am with you, says the Lord, and my spirit stands over you.
[Hag 2:4-5]

.18 And Zechariah says,

Rejoice greatly, daughter of Zion, for behold I am coming,
and I will dwell in your midst, says the Lord.
[Zech 2:14; 9:9]

.19 And again,

Behold a man, whose name is the rising, and he will rise
forth from under him. [Zech 6:12]

.20 And again,

Thus says the Lord almighty, I will return to Zion, and I
will dwell in the midst of Jerusalem, and Jerusalem will be
called a true city. [Zech 8:2-3]

.21 And Malachi says,

a. I am a great king, says the Lord almighty, and my name will
be manifested among the nations. [Mal 1:14]

b. And he will suddenly come into his temple, says the Lord
God, he whom you desire, even the angel of the covenant,
whom you seek. Behold, he is coming, says the Lord. [Mal 3:1]

[c.]   'Ανατελεῖ ὑμῖν τοῖς φοβουμένοις αὐτόν· ὄνομα αὐτοῦ
       ἥλιος δικαιοσύνης, καὶ ἴασις ἐν τοῖς πτέρυξιν
       αὐτοῦ.

[.22] Ησαΐας λέγει·

[a.]   'Εν ταῖς ἐσχάταις ἡμέραις ἐκειναῖς ἐμφανὲς ἔσται
       τὸ ὄρος Κυρίου καὶ ὁ οἶκος τοῦ θεοῦ ἐπ' ἄκρου τῶν
       ὀρέων· ἐκ Σιων ἐξελεύσεται νόμος καὶ λόγος Κυρίου
       ἐξ Ιερουσαλημ.

[b.]   Αὐτὸς Κύριος εἰς χρίσιν ἥξει μετὰ τῶν πρεσβυτέρων
       τοῦ λαοῦ.

[.23] Καὶ πάλιν·

[a.]   'Εν τῇ ἡμέρᾳ ἐκείνῃ ἐπιλάμψει ὁ θεὸς μετὰ δόξης ἐπὶ
       τῆς γῆς.

[b.]   'Εξελεύσεται ῥάβδος ἐκ τῆς ῥίζης Ιεσσαι, καὶ ἄνθος
       ἐκ τῆς ῥίζης ἀναβήσεται· καὶ ἐπαναπαύσεται ἐπ'
       αὐτὸν πνεῦμα τοῦ θεοῦ, πνεῦμα σοφίας, πνεῦμα
       συνέσεως, πνεῦμα βουλῆς καὶ ἰσχύος, πνεῦμα
       γνώσεως καὶ εὐσεβείας· καὶ ἐμπλήσει αὐτὸν πνεῦμα
       φόβου θεοῦ.

[.24] Καὶ πάλιν·

[a.]   Βασιλέα μετὰ δόξης ὄψεσθε.

[b.]   Φωνὴ βοῶντος ἐν τῇ ἐρήμῳ, ἑτοιμάσατε τὴν ὁδὸν
       Κυρίου, εὐθείας ποιεῖτε τὰς τρίβους τοῦ θεοῦ
       ἡμῶν.

[c.]   'Ιδοὺ ὁ θεὸς ἡμῶν, ἰδοὺ Κύριος μετὰ ἰσχύος
       ἔρχεται.

[.25] Καὶ πάλιν·

       Εἴπατε τῇ θυγατρὶ Σιων, ἰδοὺ ὁ σωτήρ σου παρα-
       γίνεται ἔχων τὸν ἑαυτοῦ μισθόν.

[.26] Καὶ πάλιν·

       Γνωσθήσεται ἡ χεὶρ Κυρίου τοῖς φοβουμένοις αὐτόν.

[.27] Καὶ πάλιν·

       "Εσται ἡ ῥίζα τοῦ Ιεσσαι, καὶ ὁ ἀνιστάμενος ἄρχειν
       ἐθνῶν· ἐπ' αὐτῷ ἔθνη ἐλπιοῦσι.

[.28] Καὶ πάλιν·

       'Εν σοὶ προσεύξονται, ὅτι ἐν σοὶ ὁ θεός ἐστι, καὶ
       ἐροῦσιν οὐκ ἔστι πλὴν σοῦ θεός· σὺ γὰρ εἰ θεός,
       καὶ οὐκ ᾔδειμεν.

[.29] Καὶ Ιερεμιας λέγει·

       Πνεῦμα πρὸ προσώπου ἡμῶν Χριστὸς Κύριος.

5.24b ετοιμασατε] ετοιμασαται 790.

c. He will rise up to you who fear him. His name is sun of
    righteousness, and healing is in his wings.   [Mal 3:20]

.22 Isaiah says,

a. In those last days, the mountain of the Lord will be revealed
    and the house of God will be on the top of the mountains.
    Out of Zion shall a law go forth, and the Lord's word from
    Jerusalem.   [Isa 2:2-3]

b. The Lord himself will come to judge with the elders of the
    people.   [Isa 3:14]

.23 And again,

a. In that day, God will shine with glory over the earth.
                                                          [Isa 4:2]

b. There will come forth a rod from the root of Jesse, and a
    bud will come up from the root; and the spirit of God will
    rest upon him, the spirit of wisdom, the spirit of under-
    standing, the spirit of counsel and strength, the spirit
    of knowledge and piety; and the spirit of the fear of
    God will fill him.   [Isa 11:1-3]

.24 And again,

a. You will see a king with glory.   [Isa 33:17]

b. A voice of one crying in the wilderness, prepare the way
    of the Lord, make straight the paths of our God.   [Isa 40:3]

c. Behold our God; behold the Lord is coming with strength.
                                                          [Isa 40:9-10]

.25 And again,

Say to the daughter of Zion, behold your savior comes with
his own reward.   [Isa 62:11]

.26 And again,

The hand of the Lord will be known to those who fear him.
                                                          [Isa 66:14]

.27 And again,

He will be the root of Jesse, and the one who will rise to
rule the nations. In him will the nations trust.   [Isa 11:10]

.28 And again,

They will pray through you, because God is in you, and they
will say there is no God except you; for you are God, and
we did not know it.   [Isa 45:14-15]

.29 And Jeremiah says,

The spirit before our face is the Lord Christ.   [Lam 4:20]

[.30]   Καὶ πάλιν·

         Μνήσθητί μου Κύριε καὶ ἐπίσκεφαί με· καὶ ἀθώωσόν
         με ἐκ τῶν καταδιωκόντων με.

[.31]   Καὶ πάλιν·

         Ἰδοὺ ἡμέραι ἔρχονται λέγει Κύριος, ἔρχονται, καὶ
         ἀναστήσω τῷ Δαυιδ ἀνατολὴν δικαίαν, καὶ βασιλεύσει
         βασιλεύς, καὶ συνήσει, καὶ ποιήσει κρίμα καὶ
         δικαιοσύνην ἐπὶ τῆς γῆς· ἐν ταῖς ἡμέραις αὐτοῦ
         σωθήσεται Ιουδας καὶ Ισραηλ κατασκηνώσει πεποιθὼς
         ἐπ' αὐτόν· καὶ τοῦτο τὸ ὄνομα αὐτοῦ, ὃ καλέσει
         αὐτόν Ιωσεδεκ καὶ αὐτὸς ἐν τοῖς προφήταις.

[.32]   Καὶ πάλιν·

         Γνώσονται τὸν προφήτην ὃν ἀπέστειλεν αὐτοῖς Κύριος
         ἐν πίστει.

[.33]   Καὶ πάλιν·

         Προσεύξασθε πρός με καὶ εἰσακούσομαι ὑμῶν,
         ἐκζητήσετε καὶ εὑρήσετέ με, ἐὰν ἐκζητήσετέ με
         ἐξ ὅλης καρδίας ὑμῶν, καὶ ἐπιφανοῦμαι ὑμῖν.

[.34]   Καὶ πάλιν·

         Ἐρχόμενος Κύριος ἐπ' ὄρος δίκαιον τὸ ἅγιον αὐτοῦ.

[.35]   Καὶ Ιεζεκϊηλ λέγει·

         Ἡ ὁμοίωσις τῶν προσώπων αὐτῶν τῶν τεσσάρων,
         πρόσωπον ἀνθρώπου καὶ πρόσωπον λέοντος καὶ
         πρόσωπον μόσχου καὶ πρόσωπον ἀετοῦ τοῖς τέσσαρσι.

[.36]   Καὶ πάλιν·

         Μνησθήσομαι ἐγὼ τῆς διαθήκης μου τῆς μετὰ σοῦ ἐν
         ἡμέραις νηπιότητός σου, καὶ ἀναστήσω σοι διαθήκην
         αἰώνιον· καὶ μνησθήσῃ τὴν ὁδόν σου.

[.37]   Καὶ πάλιν·

         Ἐξ ὄρους τοῦ ἁγίου μου, ἐπ' ὄρους ὑψηλοῦ, λέγει
         Κύριος, ἐκεῖ δουλεύσωσί μοι πᾶς οἶκος Ισραηλ εἰς
         τέλος.

[.38]   Καὶ πάλιν·

         Τάδε λέγει Κύριος, ἰδοὺ ἐγὼ ἐκζητήσω τὰ πρόβατά
         μου, καὶ ἐπισκέψομαι αὐτά, ὥσπερ ζητεῖ ὁ ποιμὴν
         τὸ ποίμνιον.

[.39]   Καὶ πάλιν·

         Γνώσονται ὅτι ἐγώ εἰμι κύριος ὁ θεὸς αὐτῶν, ἐν
         τῷ ἐπιφανεῖναί με αὐτοῖς ἐν τοῖς ἔθνεσι.

5.33 προσευξασθε] προσευξεσθε 790. / υμων^2] ημων 790.

.30   And again,

Remember me, Lord, and watch over me; and vindicate me
from those who persecute me.   [Jer 15:15]

.31   And again,

Behold, the days are coming, says the Lord, they are coming,
and I will raise up to David a righteous branch, and a king
will reign, and he will understand, and he will enact judgment and righteousness upon the earth. In his days Judah
will be saved and Israel will dwell securely before him.
And this is his name--he will call him Josadek and he will
be among the prophets.   [Jer 23:5-8]

.32   And again,

They will know the prophet whom the Lord has sent to them
in faithfulness.   [Jer 35:9]

.33   And again,

You will pray to me and I will listen to you; you will
earnestly seek, and you will find me if you will seek me
with your whole heart, and I will appear to you.
                                              [Jer 36:12-14]

.34   And again,

The Lord is coming on his righteous mountain, his
holy place.   [Jer 38:23]

.35   And Ezekiel says,

The likenesses of their four faces are, respectively, the
face of a man, and the face of a lion, and the face of an
ox, and the face of an eagle.   [Ezek 1:10]

.36   And again,

I will remember my covenant made with you in the days of
your infancy, and I will raise up for you an everlasting
covenant; and you will remember your way.   [Ezek 16:60-61]

.37   And again,

On my holy mountain, upon the mountain height, says the
Lord, there all the house of Israel will serve me forever.
                                              [Ezek 20:40]

.38   And again,

Thus says the Lord, behold I will seek out my sheep, and
will watch over them, as the shepherd seeks the flock.
                                              [Ezek 34:11-12]

.39   And again,

They will know that I am the Lord their God, when I have
manifested myself to them among the nations.   [Ezek 39:28]

5.40-5.52

[.40]   Καὶ Βαλααμ λέγει·

    Ἐξελεύσεται ἄνθρωπος ἐκ τοῦ σπέρματος Ισραηλ,
    καὶ κυριεύσει ἐθνῶν πολλῶν.

[.41]   Καὶ πάλιν·

    Ἀνατελεῖ ἄστρον ἐξ Ιακωβ καὶ ἀναστήσεται ἄνθρωπος
    ἐξ Ισραηλ, καὶ θραύσει τοὺς δυνατοὺς Μωαβ.

[.42]   Καὶ Δανιηλ λέγει·

    Ἕως Χριστοῦ ἡγουμένου ἑβδομάδες ἑπτὰ καὶ
    ἑβδομάδες ἑξηκονταδύο.

[.43]   Καὶ Δαυιδ λέγει·

    Ἐν τῷ ἐπιστρέψαι Κύριον τὴν αἰχμαλωσίαν τοῦ λαοῦ
    αὐτοῦ ἀγαλλιάσεται Ιακωβ καὶ εὐφρανθήσεται Ισραηλ.

[.44]   Καὶ πάλιν·

    Ὁ αὐτὸς ἐν τῷ ἡλίῳ ἔθετο τὸ σκήνωμα αὐτοῦ·
    καὶ αὐτὸς ὡς νυμφίος ἐκπορευόμενος ἐκ παστοῦ αὐτοῦ,
    ἀγαλλιάσεται ὡς γίγας δραμεῖν ὁδόν.
    ἀπ' ἄκρου τοῦ οὐρανοῦ ἡ ἔξοδος αὐτοῦ,
    καὶ τὸ κατάντημα αὐτοῦ ἕως ἄκρου τοῦ οὐρανοῦ.

[.45]   Καὶ πάλιν·

    Ἐπίφανον τὸ πρόσωπόν σου ἐπὶ τὸν δοῦλον σου.

[.46]   Καὶ πάλιν·

    Ἔκλινεν οὐρανοὺς καὶ κατέβη.

[.47]   Καὶ πάλιν·

    Ὀφθήσεται ὁ θεὸς τῶν θεῶν ἐν Σιων.

[.48]   Καὶ πάλιν·

    Εὐλογημένος ὁ ἐρχόμενος ἐν ὀνόματι Κυρίου·
    θεὸς Κύριος καὶ ἐπέφανεν ἡμῖν.

[.49]   Καὶ πάλιν·

    Παρεμβαλεῖ ἄγγελος Κυρίου κύκλῳ τῶν φοβουμένων
    αὐτον καὶ ῥύσεται αὐτούς.

[.50]   Καὶ πάλιν·

    Καταβήσεται ὡς ὑετὸς ἐπὶ πόκον.

[.51]   Καὶ πάλιν·

    Ἐγγὺς Κύριος τοῖς συντετριμμένοις τὴν καρδίαν.

[.52]   Καὶ πάλιν·

    Ἐπιφάναι τὸ πρόσωπον αὐτοῦ ἐφ' ἡμᾶς,
    καὶ ἐλεήσαι ἡμᾶς.

5.41 Ισραηλ] Ιερουσαλημ 790.
5.51 τὴν καρδιαν] τῇ καρδιᾳ 790.

.40 And Balaam says,

A man will come forth from the seed of Israel, and he will
rule over many nations. [Num 24:7]

.41 And again,

A star will rise out of Jacob and a man will spring up from
Israel, and he will crush the hosts of Moab. [Num 24:17]

.42 And Daniel says,

Until Christ the ruler there will be seven weeks and
sixty-two weeks. [Dan 9:25 (Th)]

.43 And David says,

When the Lord turns back the captivity of his people, Jacob
will exult and Israel will be glad. [Ps 13:7]

.44 And again,

He himself has set his tent in the sun,
and he is as a bridegroom coming forth out of his chamber;
he will exult as a giant to run a course.
His going forth is from the beginning of heaven
and his goal is as far as the height of heaven. [Ps 18:5-7]

.45 And again,

Reveal your face to your servant. [Ps 30:17]

.46 And again,

He bent the heavens and descended. [Ps 17:10]

.47 And again,

The God of gods will be seen in Zion. [Ps 83:8]

.48 And again,

Blessed is he who comes in the name of the Lord.
God is the Lord, and he has appeared to us. [Ps 117:26-27]

.49 And again,

An angel of the Lord will encamp all around those who fear
him, and will deliver them. [Ps 33:8]

.50 And again,

He will descend as rain on a fleece. [Ps 71:6]

.51 And again,

The Lord is near to the broken-hearted. [Ps 33:19]

.52 And again,

Let his face appear to us,
and have mercy on us. [Ps 66:2; Num 6:25]

5.53-7

[.53]   Καὶ πάλιν·

Εἴδοσαν πάντες οἱ λαοὶ
τὸ σωτηρίαν τοῦ θεοῦ ἡμῶν;

[.54]   Σολομων λέγει·

Εἰ ἀληθῶς κατοικήσει ὁ θεὸς μετὰ ἀνθρώπων.

[6]   ϛ ὅτι ὤφθη, καὶ θεὸς ὢν γέγονεν ἄνθρωπος--

[.1]   Ιερεμιας λέγει·

Οὗτος ὁ θεὸς ἡμῶν, οὐ λογισθήσεται ἕτερος πρὸς
αὐτόν. ἐξεῦρε πᾶσαν ὁδὸν ἐπιστήμης καὶ δέδωκεν
αὐτὴν Ιακωβ τῷ παιδὶ αὐτοῦ καὶ Ισραηλ τῷ
ἠγαπημένῳ ὑπ᾽ αὐτόν.

[.2]   Καὶ πάλιν·

Ἀνθρωπός ἐστι, καὶ τίς γνώσεται αὐτόν;

[.3]   Καὶ πάλιν·

Μετὰ ταῦτα ἐπὶ τῆς γῆς ὤφθη καὶ τοῖς ἀνθρώποις
συνανεστράφη.

[.4]   Καὶ Δαυιδ λέγει·

Ἀλήθεια ἐκ τῆς γῆς ἀνέτειλε.

[.5]   Καὶ πάλιν·

Καὶ ἄνθρωπος ἐγεννήθη ἐν αὐτῇ,
καὶ αὐτὸς ἐθεμελίωσεν αὐτὴν ὁ ὕψιστος.

[.6]   Ωσηε λέγει·

Σάρξ μου ἐξ αὐτῶν· τί σε διαθῶ Εφραϊμ; ὑπερασπίσω
σου Ισραηλ, διότι θεὸς ἐγώ εἰμι καὶ οὐκ ἄνθρωπος.

[.7]   Ησαϊας λέγει·

Μεθ᾽ ἡμῶν ὁ θεός, γνῶτε ἔθνη καὶ ἡττᾶσθε.

[.8]   Καὶ πάλιν·

Ἐμφανὴς ἐγενόμην τοῖς ἐμὲ μὴ ἐπερωτῶσιν, εὑρέθην
τοῖς ἐμὲ μὴ ζητοῦσιν.

[.9]   Καὶ πάλιν·

Ἐν σοὶ προσεύξονται, ὅτι ἐν σοὶ θεὸς ἐστι, καὶ
οὐκ ἔστι θεὸς πλὴν σοῦ· σὺ γὰρ εἰ θεός, καὶ οὐκ
ᾔδειμεν.

[7]   ζ ὅτι ἐκ σπέρματος Δαυιδ ὁ Κύριος--

5.53   παντες οι] σε παντες 790.
5.54   ο] om 28.
6.1   υπ] om 28.
6.8   ζητουσιν] ζητωσι 28.
6.9   ηδειμεν] ειδημεν 790.

.53 And again,

   All the people have seen
   the salvation of our God.   [Pss 96:6; 97:3]

.54 Solomon says,

   Will God really dwell with men?   [3 Kgs 8:27]

6   That he appeared, and being God became man--

.1   Jeremiah says,

   This is our God; no other will be counted as God besides him.
   He has found out the whole way of knowledge, and has given
   it to Jacob his servant and Israel whom he loves.
                                                    [Bar 3:36-37]

.2   And again,

   He is a man, and who will know him?   [Jer 17:9]

.3   And again,

   After these things, he appeared on the earth and conversed
   with men.   [Bar 3:38]

.4   And David says,

   Truth has sprung out of the earth.   [Ps 84:12]

.5   And again,

   And a man was begotten in her,
   and the most high himself has established her.   [Ps 86:5]

.6   Hosea says,

   My flesh is from them; how should I deal with you, Ephraim?
   I will protect you, Israel, for I am God and not man.
                                                    [Hos 11:8-9]

.7   Isaiah says,

   God is with us; know, nations, and be overcome.   [Isa 8:8-9]

.8   And again,

   I became visible to those who did not ask for me; I was
   found by those who did not seek me.   [Isa 65:1]

.9   And again,

   They will pray in you, because God is in you, and there is
   no God besides you; for you are God, and we did not know
   it.   [Isa 45:14-15]

7   That the Lord is from the seed of David--

7.1-11

[.1]   Δαυιδ ἐν τῷ π̄η̄ ψαλμῷ λέγει·

        Ἅπαξ ὤμοσα ἐν τῷ ἁγίῳ μου, εἰ τῷ Δαυιδ ψεύσομαι,
        τὸ σπέρμα αὐτοῦ εἰς τὸν αἰῶνα μενεῖ.

[.2]   Καὶ πάλιν·

        Ὤμοσε Κύριος τῷ Δαυιδ ἀλήθειαν καὶ οὐ μὴ ἀθετήσει
        αὐτήν·
        ἐκ καρποῦ τῆς κοιλίας σου θήσομαι ἐπὶ τὸν θρόνον σου.

[.3]   Καὶ πάλιν·

        θήσομαι εἰς τὸν αἰῶνα τοῦ αἰῶνος τὸ σπέρμα αὐτοῦ
        καὶ τὸν θρόνον αὐτοῦ ὡς τὰς ἡμέρας τοῦ οὐρανοῦ.

[.4]   Καὶ Ἡσαΐας λέγει·

        θήσω τὴν βασιλείαν αὐτοῦ ἐπὶ τὸν θρόνον Δαυιδ,
        τοῦ κατορθῶσαι αὐτὴν καὶ ἀντιλαβέσθαι ἐν δικαιο-
        σύνῃ καὶ κρίματι.

[.5]   Καὶ πάλιν Ιερεμιας·

        Ἰδοὺ ἡμέραι ἔρχονται, λέγει Κύριος, καὶ ἀναστήσω
        τῷ Δαυιδ ἀνατολὴν δικαίαν, καὶ βασιλεύσει βασιλεὺς
        καὶ συνήσει καὶ ποιήσει κρίμα καὶ δικαιοσύνην ἐπὶ
        τῆς γῆς· ἐν ταῖς ἡμέραις αὐτοῦ σωθήσεται Ισραηλ
        καὶ Ιουδας κατασκηνώσει ἐπ᾽ αὐτόν.

[8]   η̄ ὅτι ἐκ παρθένου--

        Ἡσαΐας ὁ μέγας καὶ ἔνδοξος πρῶτος βοᾷ λέγων·

        Ἰδοὺ ἡ παρθένος ἐν γαστρὶ ἔξει καὶ τέξεται υἱόν·
        καὶ καλέσουσι τὸ ὄνομα αὐτοῦ Εμμανουηλ, ὅ ἐστι
        μεθερμηνευόμενον μεθ᾽ ἡμῶν ὁ θεός.

[9]   θ̄ ὅτι μετὰ τὸ γεννηθῆναι φυλάξει τὴν τέκουσαν παρθένον--

        Ιεζεκιηλ λέγει·

        Εἶπε Κύριος πρός με· υἱὲ ἀνθρώπου, ἡ πύλη αὕτη
        κεκλεισμένη ἔσται, οὐδεὶς οὐ μὴ διέλθῃ δι᾽ αὐτῆς
        ἀλλὰ Κύριος ὁ θεὸς μόνος, καὶ εἰσελεύσεται καὶ
        καθίεται, ὅτι αὐτός ἐστιν ὁ ἡγούμενος, και
        ἐξελεύσεται καὶ κλείσει τὰς θύρας ὄπισθεν αὐτοῦ,
        καὶ ἔσται ἡ πύλη κεκλεισμένη εἰς τὸν αἰῶνα τοῦ
        αἰῶνος.

[10]   ῑ ὅτι ἡ μήτρα πύλη--

        Ιωβ λέγει·

        Διὰ τί οὐ συνέκλεισάς μοι πύλας γαστρὸς μητρός μου;

[11]   ῑᾱ ὅτι ἀνωδίνως ἡ παρθένος γεννήσει--

        Ἡσαΐας βοᾷ λέγων·

7.1 εις...μενει] μενει εις τον αιωνα 28.
7.5 παλιν] om 28.

.1 David says in the 88th Psalm,

Once I have sworn to my holy one, that I will not lie to David,
his seed will endure forever.   [Ps 88:36-37]

.2 And again,

The Lord swore in truth to David and will not annul it:
I will place on your throne someone from the fruit of your
        body.   [Ps 131:11]

.3 And again,

I will establish his seed for ever and ever,
and his throne as the days of heaven.   [Ps 88:30]

.4 And Isaiah says,

I will put his kingdom on the throne of David, to establish
it and support it in righteousness and judgment.   [Isa 9:6]

.5 And again Jeremiah,

Behold, the days are coming, says the Lord; and I will raise
up to David a righteous branch, and a king will rule and will
understand, and he will execute judgment and righteousness on
the earth. In his days Israel will be saved and Judah will
dwell near him.   [Jer 23:5-6]

8 That [he was born] from a virgin--

Isaiah the great and glorious one first cries out, saying,

Behold, the virgin will become pregnant and will bear a son;
and they will call his name Emmanuel, which means when
translated, God with us.   [Isa 7:14; Matt 1:23]

9 That after his birth, he would protect the virgin who bore [him]--

Ezekiel says,

The Lord said to me, son of man, this gate will be shut,
and no one will ever pass through it except the Lord God
alone; and he will enter and will take his seat because
he is the ruler, and he will go out and shut the doors
behind him, and the gate will be shut forever and ever.
                                      [Ezek 44:2; 46:12]

10 That the womb is a gate--

Job says,

Why did you not close to me the gates of my mother's womb?
                                               [Job 3:10-11]

11 That the virgin gave birth without travail--

Isaiah cries out, saying,

Πρίν τήν ώδίνουσαν τεκεῖν, πρὶν ἐλθεῖν τῶν
πόνων τῶν ώδίνων, ἐξέφυγε καὶ ἔτεκεν ἄρσεν.

[12]   ι̅β̅ ὅτι ἐχρίσθη--

[.1]   Δαυιδ λέγει ἐν τῷ μ̅δ̅ ψαλμῷ·

Διὰ τοῦτο ἔχρισέ σε ὁ θεὸς ὁ θεός σου ἔλαιον
ἀγαλλιάσεως παρὰ τὸν μετόχους σου.

[.2]   Καὶ Ησαΐας λέγει·

Πνεῦμα Κυρίου ἐπ’ ἐμέ, οὗ εἵνεκεν ἔχρισέ με.

[13a] ι̅γ̅ ὅτι χωρὶς πατρὸς ἐπὶ γῆς καὶ μιξέως--

[.1]   Ιερεμιας λέγει·

οἴμοι ἐγὼ μῆτερ· ὡς τίνα με τέτωκας ἄνδρα
δικαζόμενον καὶ διακρινόμενον πάσῃ τῇ γῇ.

[.2]   Καὶ Δαυιδ λέγει ἐν τῷ κ̅α̅ ψαλμῷ·

[a.]   Ὁ θεὸς ὁ θεός μου πρόσχες μοι.

[b.]   Ὅτι σὺ εἶ ὁ ἐκσπάσας με ἐκ γαστρός,
ἡ ἐλπίς μου ἀπὸ μαστῶν τῆς μητρός μου·
ἐπὶ σὲ ἐπερρίφην ἐκ μήτρας,
ἐκ κοιλίας μητρός μου θεός μου εἶ σύ.

[.3]   Καὶ Δανιηλ·

Ἐθεώρει ἕως οὗ ἀπεσχίθη λίθος ἄνευ χειρῶν,
καὶ ἐπάταξε τὴν εἰκόνα.

[13b.1] Καὶ ὅτι λίθος, Ησαΐας λέγει·

[a.]   Ἰδοὺ τίθημι λίθον προσκόμματος ἐν Σιων, καὶ
πέτραν σκανδάλου.

[b.]   Καὶ ὁ πιστεύων ἐπ’ αὐτῷ οὐ καταισχυνθήσεται.

[.2]   Καὶ Ζαχαριας λέγει·

Ἐπὶ τὸν λίθον τὸν ἕνα ἑπτὰ ὀφθαλμοὶ εἰσιν,
ἐπιβλέποντες ἐπὶ πᾶσαν τὴν γῆν.

[14]   ι̅δ̅ ὅτι παιδίον--

[.1]   Ησαΐας μαρτυρεῖ λέγων·

Ὅτι παιδίον ἐγεννήθη ἡμῖν, υἱὸς καὶ ἐδόθη ἡμῖν,
οὗ ἡ ἀρχὴ ἐπὶ τοῦ ὤμου αὐτοῦ, καὶ καλεῖται τὸ
ὄνομα αὐτοῦ μεγάλης βουλῆς ἄγγελος.

[.2]   Καὶ πάλιν ὁ αὐτὸς λέγει·

Πρὶν γνῶναι τὸ παιδίον καλεῖν πατέρα ἢ μητέρα
αὐτοῦ, ἔλαβε τὴν δύμανιν Δαμασκοῦ.

[.3]   Καὶ πάλιν·

Παιδίον μικρὸν γράψει αὐτούς.

12.2 ειvεκεν] ενεκεν 28, ηνεκεν 790.

Before the woman in labor could bear, before she experienced
the pains of labor, she escaped [them] and gave birth to a
male.   [Isa 66:7]

12   That he was anointed--

.1   In the 44th Psalm, David says,

Therefore God, your God, anointed you
with the oil of gladness beyond your companions.   [Ps 44:8]

.2   And Isaiah says,

The spirit of the Lord is upon me, for which reason he has
anointed me.   [Isa 61:1]

13a That without a father on earth or intercourse [he was born]--

.1   Jeremiah says,

Woe is me, mother. You have borne me like some man condemned
and judged by all the earth.   [Jer 15:10]

.2   And in the 21st Psalm, David says,

a. O God, my God, pay attention to me.   [Ps 21:2]

b. Because you are the one who drew me from the womb,
my hope from my mother's breasts;
I was cast on you from the womb,
From my mother's womb you are my God.   [Ps 21:10-11]

.3   And Daniel,

He looked until a stone was cut out without hands, and it
struck down the image.   [Dan 2:34 (Th)]

13b.1 And that he is a stone, Isaiah says,

a. Behold, I am laying a stone of stumbling in Zion, and a rock
of offense.   [Isa 8:14; Rom 9:33]

b. And whoever believes in him will not be put to shame.
[Isa 28:16; Rom 9:33]

.2   And Zechariah says,

On the one stone are seven eyes, looking upon all the earth.
[Zech 3:9; 4:10]

14   That he was a child--

.1   Isaiah witnesses, saying,

A child is born to us, and a son is given to us, on whose
shoulder the government will rest, and his name will be
called the messenger of great counsel.   [Isa 9:5]

.2   And again the same one says,

Before the child knew enough to call his father or mother,
he received the host of Damascus.   [Isa 8:4]

.3   And again,

A little child will write them.   [Isa 10:19]

[15]   ιε ὅτι ἐν Βηθλεεμ τεχθήσεται--

         Ησαῖας λέγει·

         Οἰκήσει ἐν ὑψηλῷ τόπῳ ἐπὶ πέτρας ὀχυράς.

[16]   ις ὅτι προσκυνήσουσιν οἱ μάγοι--

   [.1]   Δαυιδ ἐν τῷ οα ψαλμῷ λέγει·

         Βασιλεῖς θαρσεῖς καὶ νῆσοι δῶρα προσοίσουσι,
         βασιλεῖς 'Αράβων καὶ Σαβα δῶρα προσάξουσι·
         καὶ προσκυνήσουσιν αὐτῷ πάντες οἱ βασιλεῖς τῆς γῆς.

   [.2]   Καὶ Ησαῖας λέγει·

         "Ηξουσιν ἐκ Σαβα φέροντες χρυσίον καὶ λίβανον καὶ
         σμύρναν, καὶ εὐαγγελιοῦνται τὸ σωτήριον τοῦ Κυρίου.

[17]   ιζ ὅτι ἀνατελεῖ ὁ ἀστήρ--

         Βαλααμ λέγει·

   [a.]   'Ανατελεῖ ἄστρον ἐξ Ιακωβ,
         καὶ ἀναστήσεται ἄνθρωπος ἐξ Ισραηλ.

   [b.]   Καὶ ὑψωθήσεται ἡ βασιλεία αὐτοῦ.

[18]   ιη ὅτι τὰ βρέφη ἀναιρεθήσονται--

         Ιερεμιας οὕτως θρηνεῖ λέγων·

         Οὕτως εἶπε Κύριος, φωνὴ ἐν Ραμα ἠκούσθη θρῆνος
         καὶ οὐαὶ καὶ κλαυθμὸς καὶ ὀδυρμός· Ραχηλ
         ἀποκλαιομένη οὐκ ἠθέλησε παύσασθαι ἐπὶ τῶν υἱῶν,
         ὅτι οὐκ εἰσίν. οὕτως εἶπε Κύριος, διαλειπέτω ἡ
         φωνή σου ἀπὸ κλαυθμοῦ καὶ οἱ ὀφθαλμοί σου ἀπὸ
         δακρύων σου ὅτι ὁ μισθὸς τοῖς σοῖς ἔργοις, καὶ
         ἐπιστρέψουσιν ἐκ γῆς ἐχθρῶν, μονίμοις τοῖς σοῖς
         τέκνοις.

[19]   ιθ ὅτι ταραχθήσεται Ηρῳδης καὶ οἱ μετ' αὐτοῦ πάντες--

         Ιερεμιας λέγει·

         'Εν τῇ ἡμέρᾳ ἐκείνῃ, λέγει Κύριος, ἀπολεῖται ἡ
         καρδία τοῦ βασιλέως καὶ ἡ καρδίαν τῶν ἀρχόντων,
         καὶ οἱ ἱερεῖς ἐκστήσονται, καὶ οἱ προφῆται
         θαυμάσονται.

[20]   κ ὅτι ὑποκρίσει ζητήσει προσκυνῆσαι--

         Δαυιδ λέγει ἐν τῷ ξε ψαλμῷ·

         'Εν τῷ πλήθει τῆς δυνάμεώς σου ψεύσονται οἱ ἐχθροί
         σου.

16.1 Αραβων] Αρραβων 790.
16.2 του] om 790.
18   σου³] om 28.
19   ιερεις] ιεροις 28.

15 That he would be born in Bethlehem--

Isaiah says,

He will live in a high place on firm rock.   [Isa 33:16]

16 That the magi would worship him--

.1 In the 71st Psalm, David says,

Kings of Tharsis and the isles will bring gifts,
kings of the Arabs and Saba will offer gifts;
and all the kings of the earth will worship him. [Ps 71:10-11]

.2 And Isaiah says,

They will come from Saba bearing gold and frankincense and
myrrh, and they will proclaim the salvation of the Lord.
                                              [Isa 60:6; Matt 2:11]

17 That the star would rise--

Balaam says,

a. A star will rise out of Jacob,
   and a man will spring out of Israel.   [Num 24:17]

b. And his kingdom will be exalted.   [Num 24:7]

18 That the infants would be slaughtered--

Jeremiah laments thus, saying,

Thus said the Lord: a voice was heard in Rama, lamentation
and woe and weeping and wailing. Rachel would not stop
weeping for her sons, because they are not. Thus says the
Lord: let your voice cease from weeping and your eyes from
your tears, for there will be a reward for your works, and
they will return from the land of the enemies, to abodes
that will be secure for your children.   [Jer 38:15-17]

19 That Herod would be disturbed, and all those with him--

Jeremiah says,

In that day, says the Lord, the heart of the king will
perish, and the heart of the rulers; and the priests will be
amazed and the prophets will wonder.   [Jer 4:9]

20 That with hypocrisy, [Herod] would seek to worship [him]--

In the 65th Psalm, David says,

In the greatness of your power your enemies will be false.
                                                [Ps 65:3]

[21]   κ̄ᾱ   ὅτι θυμωθήσεται ἀπατηθείς--

              Δαυιδ ἐν τῷ ρ̄ῑᾱ φαλμῷ λέγει·

                   'Αμαρτωλὸς ὄψεται καὶ ὀργισθήσεται,
                   τοὺς ὀδόντας αὐτοῦ βρύξει καὶ τακήσεται.

[22]   κ̄β̄   ὅτι ἐρευνήσει καὶ ἀναζητήσει--

              Δαυιδ λέγει ἐν τῷ ξ̄γ̄ φαλμῷ·

                   Εἶπαν τίς ὄψεται αὐτούς,
                   ἢ διηγήσεται τοῦ κρύψαι παγίδας;
                   ἐξέλιπον ἐξερευνῶντες ἐξερευνήσει.

[23]   κ̄γ̄   ὅτι ἀνελεῖ τὰ βρέφη--

              'Ερρέθη ἐν τῷ ῑη̄ κεφαλαίῳ.

[24]   κ̄δ̄   ὅτι οὐκ ἀνελεῖ τὸν Χριστόν--

   [.1]   Δαυιδ λέγει ἐν τῷ λ̄ς̄ φαλμῷ·

                   Κατανοεῖ ὁ ἁμαρτωλὸς τὸν δίκαιον
                   τοῦ ἀπολέσαι αὐτόν,
                   ὁ δὲ Κύριος οὐ μὴ ἐγκαταλείπῃ αὐτὸν εἰς τὰς
                        χεῖρας αὐτοῦ.

   [.2]   Καὶ πάλιν ἐν τῷ ρ̄ῑᾱ φαλμῷ·

                   'Επιθυμία ἁμαρτωλῶν ἀπολεῖται.

[25]   κ̄ε̄   ὅτι εἰς Αἴγυπτον καταβήσεται ὁ Χριστός--

   [.1]   Ησαΐας λέγει·

                   'Ιδοὺ Κύριος κάθηται ἐπὶ νεφέλης κούφης καὶ
                   ἥξει εἰς Αἴγυπτον, καὶ σεισθήσονται πάντα τὰ
                   χειροποίητα Αἰγύπτου.

   [.2]   Καὶ πάλιν·

                   Γνωσθήσεται Κύριος τοῖς Αἰγυπτίοις, καὶ
                   φοβηθήσονται οἱ Αἰγύπτιοι τὸν Κύριον ἐν τῇ
                   ἡμέρᾳ ἐκείνῃ.

[26]   κ̄ς̄   ὅτι ἐξ Αἰγύπτου κληθήσεται--

   [.1]   Ιωηλ λέγει·

                   'Εξ Αἰγύπτου ἐκάλεσα τὸν υἱόν μου.

   [.2]   Καὶ Βαλααμ λέγει·

                   'Ο θεὸς ὡδήγησεν αὐτὸν ἐξ Αἰγύπτου,
                   ὡς δόξαν μονοκέρωτος αὐτοῦ.

---

21 θυμωθησεται] θημωθησεται 790.
21 αυτου] αυτους 790.
22 ειπαν] om 790. / διηγησεται] διηγησετο 28.
23 κ̄γ̄...κεφαλαιψ] lower margin 790, om 28.

21 That when [Herod] was deceived he would become angry--

    In the 111th Psalm, David says,

        The sinner will see and be angry;
        he will gnash his teeth and waste away.   [Ps 111:10]

22 That [Herod] would search and look [for him]--

    In the 63d Psalm, David says,

        Say, who will see them,
        or will give advice to hide snares?
        They have wearied themselves by searching diligently.
                                                    [Ps 63:6-7]

23 That [Herod] would put the infants to death--

    It was quoted in the 18th section.

24 That [Herod] would not put the Christ to death--

    .1 In the 36th Psalm, David says,

        The sinner spies on the righteous
        in order to kill him,
        but the Lord will not abandon him to his hands.   [Ps 36:32]

    .2 And again in the 111th Psalm,

        The desire of the sinners will perish.   [Ps 111:10]

25 That the Christ would go down into Egypt--

    .1 Isaiah says,

        Behold, the Lord sits on a swift cloud and he will come to
        Egypt, and all the temples of Egypt will be shaken. [Isa 19:1]

    .2 And again,

        The Lord will be known to the Egyptians, and the
        Egyptians will fear the Lord in
        that day.   [Isa 19:21]

26 That he would be called out of Egypt--

    .1 Joel says,

        Out of Egypt have I called my son.   [Hos 11:1; Matt 2:15]

    .2 And Balaam says,

        God led him out of Egypt,
        as the glory of his unicorn.   [Num 24:8]

[27] κζ ὅτι βαπτιζόμενος ἁγιάσει τὰ ὕδατα--

Ιεζεκιηλ λέγει ἰδών·

[a.] Ἰδοὺ ὕδωρ καταφερόμενον ἀπὸ τοῦ κλίτους τοῦ
δεξιοῦ· καὶ ἐγένετο καθὼς ἔξοδος ἀνδρὸς ἡ ἔξοδος
αὐτοῦ. καὶ διῆλθεν ἐν τῷ ὕδατι ὕδωρ ἀφέσεως.

[b.] Καὶ εἶπε Κύριος πρός με· υἱὲ ἀνθρώπου, τοῦτο τὸ
ὕδωρ τὸ πορευόμενον ἐπὶ γῆν Γαλιλαίαν ἁγιάσει τὰ
ὕδατα· καὶ ἔσται πᾶσα ψυχὴ ἐφ᾽ ἣ ἂν ἐπέλθῃ τὸ
ὕδωρ τοῦτο ζησέται καὶ ἰαθήσεται.

[28] κη ὅτι ἐνδόξως ἀπὸ τοῦ βαπτίσματος ἀναβήσεται--

Ιερεμιας λέγει·

Ἰδοὺ ὡς λέων ἀναβήσεται ἐκ μέσου τοῦ Ιορδάνου.

[29] κθ ὅτι ἐπὶ θαλάσσης περιπατήσει--

Ιωβ λέγει·

Ὁ τανύσας τὸν οὐρανὸν μόνος,
ὁ περιπατῶν ἐπὶ θαλάσσης ὡς ἐπὶ ἐδάφους.

[30] λ ὅτι τὸ κράσπεδον τοῦ ἱματίου αὐτοῦ θεραπεύσει--

Μαλαχιας λέγει·

Ἀνατελεῖ τοῖς φοβουμένοις τὸ ὄνομα αὐτου ἥλιος
δικαιοσύνης ἔχων ἴασιν ἐν ταῖς πτέρυξιν.

[31] λα ὅτι ξηρανεῖ τὴν συκῆν--

[.1] Αβακουμ λέγει·

Διότι συκῆ οὐ καρποφορήσει.

[.2] Καὶ Ιεζεκιηλ λέγει·

Ἐγὼ Κύριος ὁ ξηρῶν ξύλον χλωρόν.

[32] λβ ὅτι πειρασθήσεται ὑπὸ τοῦ διαβόλου--

[.1] Ζαχαριας λέγει·

Καὶ ἔδειξέ μοι Κύριος Ἰησοῦν τὸν ἱερέα τὸν μέγαν
ἐστῶτα πρὸ προσώπου ἀγγέλου Κυρίου, καὶ ὁ διάβολος
εἰστήκει ἐκ δεξιῶν αὐτοῦ τοῦ ἀντικεῖσθαι αὐτῷ.
καὶ εἶπεν αὐτῷ ὁ Κύριος· ἐπιτιμήσαι σοὶ Κύριος,
διάβολε, ὁ ἐκλεξάμενος τὴν Ιερουσαλημ.

[.2] Καὶ αὐτὸς δὲ ὁ Κύριος περὶ ἑαυτοῦ λέγων εἶπε πρὸς Ιωβ·

Οὐχ ἑώρακας αὐτόν
οὐδε ἐπὶ τοῖς λεγομένοις τεθαύμακας;

---

30   το] του 28.
31.1 Αβακουμ] ὁ Αβακουμ 28.
32.1 ειστηκει] εστηκει 28.

27 That when he is baptized, he would sanctify the waters--

Ezekiel says, in a vision,

a. Behold, water coming down from the cliff on the right, and
its going forth was like the going forth of a man, and the
water of forgiveness spread out in the water.   [Ezek 47:2-3]

b. And the Lord said to me, son of man, this water which flows
on the land of Galilee will sanctify the waters, and it will
happen that every soul on which this water comes will live
and will be healed.   [Ezek 47:8-9]

28 That he would ascend from his baptism gloriously--

Jeremiah says,

Behold, he will come up as a lion from the middle of the
Jordan.   [Jer 30:13]

29 That he would walk on the sea--

Job says,

He who has stretched out the heaven alone,
he who walks on the sea as on firm ground.   [Job 9:8]

30 That the hem of his garment would heal--

Malachi says,

To those who fear his name, the sun of righteousness rises
having healing in his wings.   [Mal 3:20]

31 That he would wither the fig tree--

.1 Habakkuk says,

For the fig tree will bear no fruit.   [Hab 3:17]

.2 And Ezekiel says,

I am the Lord who withers the green tree.   [Ezek 17:24]

32 That he would be tempted by the devil--

.1 Zechariah says,

And the Lord showed me Jesus the high priest standing before
the face of the angel of the Lord, and the devil stood on
his right hand to oppose him. And the Lord said to him, the
Lord who has chosen Jerusalem rebuke you, devil. [Zech 3:1-2]

.2 And the Lord himself, speaking about himself, said to Job,

Have you not seen him,
and have you not wondered about the things said?

οὐ δέδοικας ὅτι ἡτοίμασταί μοι;
τίς γάρ ἐστιν ὁ ἐμοὶ ἀντιστάς;
ἢ τίς ἀντιστήσεταί με καὶ ὑπομενεῖ;

[33]   λγ ὅτι θεραπεύσει πολλούς--

    [.1]   Ἡσαΐας λέγει·

           Ἰσχυσᾶτε χεῖρες ἀνειμέναι καὶ γόνατα παραλελυμένα·
           παρακαλέσατε ὀλιγόψυχοι τῇ διανοίᾳ· μή φοβηθῆτε.

    [.2]   Καὶ πάλιν·

           Ὁ θεὸς τότε ἥξει· τότε ἀνοιχθήσονται ὀφθαλμοὶ
           τυφλῶν, καὶ ὦτα κωφῶν ἀκούσονται· τότε ἁλιεῖται
           ὡς ἔλαφος ὁ χωλός, καὶ τρανὴ ἔσται γλῶσσα
           μογιλάλων.

[34]   λδ ὅτι ἀναστήσει νεκρούς--

           Ἡσαΐας λέγει·

           Κατέπιεν ὁ θάνατος ἰσχύσας, καὶ πάλιν ἀφεῖλεν ὁ θεὸς
           πᾶν δάκρυον ἀπὸ παντὸς προσώπου.

[35]   λε ὅτι ἀπιστήσουσιν οἱ Ἰουδαῖοι--

           Ἡσαΐας λέγει·

    [a.]   Κύριε, τίς ἐπίστευσε τῇ ἀκοῇ ἡμῶν; καὶ ὁ βραχίων
           Κυρίου τίνι ἀπεκαλύφθη;

    [b.]   Ὄψονται οἷς οὐκ ἀνηγγέλη περὶ αὐτοῦ, καὶ οἳ οὐκ
           ἀκηκόασι συνήσουσιν.

[36]   λς ὅτι ἀπὸ ε ἄρτων θρέψει πολλούς--

           Ἡσαΐας λέγει·

           Ἐροῦσιν ἐν τῇ ἡμέρα ἐκείνῃ· ἰδού ὁ θεός ἡμῶν·
           ἠλπίζομεν καὶ ἠγαλλιασάμεθα ἐπὶ τῷ σωτηρίῳ ἡμῶν, ὅτι
           ἀνάπαυσιν δώσει ὁ θεὸς ἐπὶ τὸ ὄρος τοῦτο.

[37]   λζ ὅτι ἐπὶ ὄνου εἰς τὴν Σιων ἐπελεύσεται--

    [.1]   Ζαχαριας λέγει·

           Χαῖρε σφόδρα θύγατερ Σιων, κήρυσσε θύγατερ
           Ιερουσαλημ, ὅτι ὁ βασιλεύς σου ἔρχεταί σοι
           δίκαιος καὶ πραΰς καὶ ἐπιβεβηκὼς ἐπὶ ὑποζύγιον
           καὶ πῶλον νέον.

    [.2]   Καὶ Ιακωβ λέγει·

           Δεσμεύων πρὸς ἄμπελον τὴν ὄνον αὐτοῦ.

33.1   ισχυσατε] ισχυσαται 790, ισχυσατ 28.
33.2   μογιλαλων] μογγιλαλων 28, μογκιλαλων 790.
36   ηγαλλιασαμεθα] ηγαλλιασωμεθα 28.
37.1   οτι] διο 28.

Do you not fear that he is prepared for me?
For who is the one who resists me?
Or who will resist me and survive?   [Job 41:1-3]

33 That he would heal many--

.1 Isaiah says,

Be strong, withered hands and palsied knees; you who are
spiritually discouraged be comforted. Do not fear.
[Isa 35:3-4]

.2 And again,

Then God will come; then the eyes of the blind will be
opened, and the ears of the deaf will hear; then the lame
man will leap like a deer, and the tongues of the dumb will
enunciate clearly.   [Isa 35:4-6]

34 That he would raise the dead--

Isaiah says,

Death, having prevailed, swallowed [them] up, and again God
wiped away every tear from every face.   [Isa 25:8]

35 That the Jews would be disbelieving--

Isaiah says,

a. Lord, who has believed our report? And to whom has the arm
of the Lord been revealed?   [Isa 53:1]

b. Those to whom there was no report about him will see, and
those who have not heard will consider.   [Isa 52:15]

36 That from five loaves [of bread] he would feed many--

Isaiah says,

In that day they will say, behold our God; we hoped and
rejoiced in our salvation, because God will give rest on
this mountain.   [Isa 25:9-10]

37 That on an ass he would come into Zion--

.1 Zechariah says,

Rejoice greatly, daughter of Zion; proclaim, daughter of
Jerusalem, that your king is coming to you, righteous and
meek, and mounted on an ass and a young foal.   [Zech 9:9]

.2 And Jacob says,

Binding his donkey to a vine.   [Gen 49:11]

[.3]   Καὶ Μαλαχιας λέγει·
            Ἐξαίφνης ἥξει εἰς τὸν ναὸν αὐτοῦ Κύριος, ὃν ὑμεῖς
            θέλετε, καὶ ὁ ἄγγελος τῆς διαθήκης.

[38]   λη ὅτι τὰ βρέφη προδράμουσι κράζοντα τὸ εὐλογήμενος ὁ
            ἐρχόμενος--
            Δαυιδ ἐν τῷ η̅ ψαλμῷ λέγει·
            Ἐκ στόματος νηπίων καὶ θηλαζόντων κατηρτίσω αἶνον.

[39]   λθ ὅτι ἐλέγξει τὸν λαόν--
[.1]   Μαλαχιας λέγει·
            Προσάξω πρὸς ὑμᾶς ἐν κρίσει καὶ ἔσομαι μάρτυς
            ταχὺς ἐπὶ τοὺς φαρμακοὺς καὶ ἐπὶ τὰς μοιχαλίδας
            καὶ ἐπὶ τοὺς ὀμνύοντας ἐπὶ ψεύσμασι.

[.2]   Καὶ Ιερεμιας λέγει·
            Μὴ σπήλαιον λῃστῶν ὁ οἶκος μου ἐστι; καὶ ἐπικέκ-
            ληται τὸ ὄνομά μου ἐπ’ αὐτοῖς;

[40]   μ   ὅτι ἐπιχυθήσεται αὐτῷ νάρδος--
            Ἐν τοῖς Ἄσμασι λέγει·
            Ἕως οὐ βασιλεὺς ἐν ἀνακλίσει αὐτοῦ
            νάρδος ἔδωκεν ὀσμήν αὐτοῦ.

[41]   μα ὅτι συναχθήσονται κατ’ αὐτοῦ--
[.1]   Δαυιδ ἐν τῷ β̅ ψαλμῷ λέγει·
            Ἵνα τί ἐρρύαξαν ἔθνη
            καὶ λαοὶ ἐμελέτησαν κενά;
            παρέστησαν οἱ βασιλεῖς τῆς γῆς,
            καὶ οἱ ἄρχοντες συνήχθησαν ἐπὶ τὸ αὐτὸ
            κατὰ τοῦ Κυρίου καὶ κατὰ τοῦ Χριστοῦ αυτῶν.

[.2]   Καὶ πάλιν ἐν τῷ γ̅ ψαλμῷ λέγει·
            Κύριε, τί ἐπληθύνθησαν οἱ θλίβοντές με;
            πολλοὶ ἐπανίστανται ἐπ’ ἐμέ·
            πολλοὶ λέγουσι τῇ ψυχῇ μου·
            οὐκ ἔστι σωτηρία αὐτοῦ ἐν τῷ θεῷ αὐτοῦ.

[.3]   Καὶ Ιερεμιας λέγει·
            Πνεῦμα πρὸ προσώπου ἡμῶν Χριστὸς Κύριος συνελήφθη
            ἐν ταῖς διαφθοραῖς ἡμῶν, οὐ εἴπαμεν· ἐν τῇ σκιᾷ
            αὐτοῦ ζησόμεθα.

---

38   ευλογημενος ο ερχομενος] ευλογ ο 28. / νηπιων] νηπιον 790.
41.1 παρεστησαν...αυτων] om 790.
41.2 επανισταντai] επανεσησαν 28.
41.3 ειπαμεν] ειπομεν 28.

.3 · And Malachi says,

> The Lord whom you desire will come suddenly into his
> temple, even the messenger of the covenant.   [Mal 3:1]

38 That the infants would run ahead, crying out, "Blessed is he who
comes"--

> In the 8th Psalm, David says,

> Out of the mouth of babes and sucklings you have ordained
>   praise.   [Ps 8:3]

39 That he would reprove the people--

.1 Malachi says,

> I will draw near to you in judgment, and I will be a swift
> witness against the magicians and against the adulteresses
> and against those who swear falsely.   [Mal 3:5]

.2 And Jeremiah says,

> My house is not a den of robbers, is it? And is my name
> placed on them?   [Jer 7:11]

40 That oil of nard would be poured over him--

> In the [Song of] Songs it says,

> As long as the king was reclining at his place,
> nard gave off its odor.   [Cant 1:12]

41 That they would come together against him--

.1 In the 2d Psalm, David says,

> Why do the nations rage
> and the peoples imagine empty things?
> The kings of the earth arose,
> and the rulers were gathered together
> against the Lord and against their Christ.   [Ps 2:1-2]

.2 And again, in the 3d Psalm he says,

> Lord, why are there so many who afflict me?
> Many rise against me;
> many say to my soul,
> there is no salvation for him in his God.   [Ps 3:2-3]

.3 And Jeremiah says,

> The breath before our face, the Lord Christ, was taken in
> our destructive snares, of whom we said, in his shadow we
> will live.   [Lam 4:20]

41.4-44

[.4] Καὶ πάλιν λέγει·

Ὅτι ἐνεχείρισαν λόγους εἰς σύλληψίν μου καὶ
παγίδας ἔκριψάν μοι. Καὶ σύ, Κύριε, ἔγνως πᾶσαν
αὐτῶν τὴν βουλὴν ἐπ' ἐμὲ εἰς θάνατον· μὴ ἀθῴωσῃς
τὰς ἀδικίας αὐτῶν, καὶ τὰς ἁμαρτίας αὐτῶν ἀπὸ
προσώπου μὴ ἐξαλείψῃς.

[42] μβ̄ ὅτι καταφευδομαρτυρήσουσι--

[.1] Δαυιδ ἐν τῷ λδ̄ ψαλμῷ λέγει·

Ἀναστάντες μοι μάρτυρες ἄδικοι ἃ οὐκ ἐγίνωσκον
ἠρώτων με·
ἀνταπεδίδοσάν μοι πονηρὰ ἀντὶ ἀγαθῶν.

[.2] Καὶ πάλιν ἐν τῷ νη̄ ψαλμῷ λέγει·

Ἐξελοῦ με ἐκ τῶν ἐχθρῶν μου, ὁ θεός,
καὶ ἐκ τῶν ἐπανισταμένων ἐπ' ἐμὲ λύτρωσαί με·
ῥῦσαί με ἐκ τῶν ἐργαζομένων τὴν ἀνομίαν
καὶ ἐξ ἀνδρῶν αἱμάτων σῶσόν με.

[43] μγ̄ ὅτι Ιουδας προδώσει--

[.1] Δαυιδ ἐν τῷ μ̄ ψαλμῷ λέγει·

Οἱ ἐχθροί μου εἶπον κακά μοι·
πότε ἀποθανεῖται καὶ ἀπολεῖται τὸ ὄνομα αὐτοῦ;
καὶ εἰσεπορεύετο τοῦ ἰδεῖν, μάτην ἐλάλει·
ἡ καρδία αὐτοῦ συνήγαγεν ἀνομίαν ἑαυτῷ,
ἐξεπορεύετο ἔξω καὶ ἐλάλει.
ἐπι τὸ αὐτὸ κατ' ἐμοῦ ἐψιθύριζον πάντες οἱ ἐχθροί
    μου,
κατ' ἐμοῦ ἐλογίζοντο κακά μοι,
λόγον παράνομον κατέθεντο κατ' ἐμοῦ.

[.2] Καὶ πάλιν·

Ὁ ἐσθίων ἄρτους μου ἐμεγάλυνεν ἐπ' ἐμὲ πτερνισμόν.

[.3] Καὶ πάλιν ἐν τῷ νᾱ ψαλμῷ λέγει·

Τί ἐγκαυχᾷ ἐν κακίᾳ, ὁ δυνατός,
ἀνομίαν ὅλην τὴν ἡμέραν;
ἀδικίαν ἐλογίσατο ἡ γλῶσσά σου·
ὡσεὶ ξυρὸν ἠκονημένον ἐποίησας δόλον·
ἠγάπησας κακίαν ὑπὲρ ἀγαθοσύνην.

[.4] Καὶ πάλιν ἐν τῷ λζ̄ ψαλμῷ λέγει·

Οἱ φίλοι μου καὶ οἱ πλησίον μου ἐξ ἐναντίας μου
ἤγγισαν καὶ ἔστησαν.

[44] μδ̄ ὅτι ἐρεῖ ὁ Ιουδας· χαῖρε ῥαββί--

41.4 λεγει] om 790.
43.1 ιδειν] om 28. / κατ'...μοι] om 28.
43.3 ολην...σου] ελογισατο η γλωσσα σου αδικιαν ολην την ημεραν 28.
44   ο] om 28. / ραββι] ραμβι 790.

.4 And again he says,

> For they have formed plans to take me, and have hidden
> snares for me. And you, Lord, knowing all their counsel
> against me to bring death, do not render their iniquities
> guiltless, and do not blot their sins from your face.
>   [Jer 18:22-23]

42 That they would bear false witness against him--

.1 In the 34th Psalm, David says,

> Unjust witnesses arose against me, asking me things which I
>   did not know;
> they repaid me evil for good.   [Ps 34:11-12]

.2 And again, in the 58th Psalm he says,

> Deliver me from my enemies, God,
> and ransom me from those who rise up against me;
> deliver me from those working iniquity
> and save me from bloody men.   [Ps 58:2-3]

43 That Judas would betray [him]--

.1 In the 40th Psalm, David says,

> My enemies have spoken evil against me:
> when will he die and his name perish?
> And he came to see [me], he spoke empty words;
> his heart gathered iniquity to itself,
> he went forth and spoke.
> All my enemies whispered together against me,
> and against me they devised evil;
> they laid down an evil word against me.   [Ps 40:6-9]

.2 And again,

> He who ate my bread lifted up his heel against me. [Ps 40:10]

.3 And again in the 51st Psalm, he says,

> Why, mighty one, do you evilly boast
> of iniquity the whole day?
> Your tongue has devised iniquity;
> you have devised deceit that is like a sharp razor.
> You have loved evil more than goodness.   [Ps 51:3-5]

.4 And again, in the 37th Psalm he says,

> My friends and my neighbors drew near and took their stand
> opposite me.   [Ps 37:12]

44 That Judas would say, "Hail, Rabbi"--

44.1-47.3

[.1]   Δαυιδ ἐν τῷ ν̅δ̅ ψαλμῷ λέγει·

'Ηπαλύνθησαν οἱ λόγοι αυτοῦ ὑπὲρ ἔλαιον,
καὶ αὐτοί εἰσι βολίδες.
ἐπίρριφον ἐπὶ Κύριον τὴν μέριμνάν σου, καὶ αὐτός
σε διαθρέψει.

[.2]   Καὶ πάλιν ὁ αὐτὸς ἐν τῷ ρ̅η̅ ψαλμῷ λέγει·

'Ο Θεὸς τὴν αἴνεσίν μου μὴ παρασιωπήσῃς,
ὅτι στόμα ἁμαρτωλοῦ καὶ στόμα δολίου ἐπ' ἐμὲ
ἠνοίχθη.

[45]   μ̅ε̅   ὅτι ἀργυρίου πραθήσεται--

[.1]   Ζαχαριας λέγει·

'Ερῶ πρὸς αὐτούς· εἰ καλὸν ἐνώπιον ὑμῶν, δότε τὸν
μισθόν μου τριάκοντα ἀργύρια.

[.2]   Καὶ Ιερεμιας λέγει·

"Εδωκαν τὰ τριάκοντα ἀργύρια τὴν τιμὴν τοῦ
τετιμημένου ὃν ἐτιμήσαντο ἀπὸ υἱῶν Ισραηλ· καὶ
ἔδωκαν αὐτὰ εἰς τὸν ἀγρὸν τοῦ κεραμέως.

[46]   μ̅ς̅   ὅτι δήσουσιν αὐτόν--

[.1]   Ησαϊας λέγει·

Οὐαὶ τῇ ψυχῇ ὑμῶν, ὅτι ἐβουλεύσαντο βουλὴν πονηρὰν
καθ' ἑαυτῶν εἰπόντες· ὅτι δήσωμεν ἄνδρα δίκαιον,
ὅτι δύσχρηστος ἡμῖν ἐστι.

[.2]   Καὶ Σολομων λέγει·

'Ενεδρεύσωμεν τὸν δίκαιον, ὅτι δύσχρηστος ἡμιν ἐστι·
βαρὺς ἡμῖν ἐστι καὶ βλεπόμενος.

[47]   μ̅ζ̅   ὅτι κρίνουσιν αὐτόν--

[.1]   Δαυιδ ἐν τῷ ξ̅η̅ ψαλμῷ λέγει·

Σῶσόν με, ὁ Θεός, ὅτι εἰσήλθοσαν ὕδατα ἕως ψυχῆς μου.
ἐνεπάγην εἰς ἰλὺν βυθοῦ, καὶ οὐκ ἔστιν ὑπόστασις.

[.2]   Καὶ πάλιν ὁ αὐτὸς ἐν τῷ ο̅ ψαλμῷ λέγει·

'Επὶ σοί, Κύριε, ἤλπισα, μὴ καταισχυνθείην εἰς τὸν
αἰῶνα.
ἐν τῇ δικαιοσύνῃ σου ῥῦσαί με καὶ ἐξελοῦ με.

Καὶ τὰ ἑξῆς.

[.3]   Καὶ Ησαϊας λέγει·

44.1   αυτου] αυτων 790.
45.1   αργυρια] αργυριους 28.
46.1   ανδρα] τον 28.
47.1   ιλυν] ολην 28.

.1 In the 54th Psalm, David says,

His words were smoother than oil,
and they are darts.
Cast your care upon the Lord, and he will sustain you.
[Ps 54:22-23]

.2 And again, in the 108th Psalm the same one says,

God, do not pass over my praise in silence,
for the mouth of the sinner and the mouth of the crafty
have opened against me.   [Ps 108:1-2]

45 That he would be sold for silver--

.1 Zechariah says,

I will say to them, If it is good in your judgment, give me
my price--thirty pieces of silver.   [Zech 11:12]

.2 And Jeremiah says,

They gave the thirty pieces of silver, the price of him on
whom a price had been set, whom they priced from the sons of
Israel; and they gave them for the potter's field.
[Zech 11:13; Matt 27:9-10; (Jer 39:6-9)]

46 That they would bind him--

.1 Isaiah says,

Woe to your soul, for they have devised evil counsel against
themselves, saying, Let us bind the just man, because he is
burdensome to us.   [Isa 3:9-10]

.2 And Solomon says,

Let us lie in wait for the righteous, because he is
burdensome to us;
he is troublesome to us even to look at.   [Wis 2:12; 14]

47 That they would judge him--

.1 In the 68th Psalm, David says,

Save me, God, because waters have come up over my soul.
I am stuck fast in deep mire, and there is no standing.
[Ps 68:2-3]

.2 And again, in the 70th Psalm the same one says,

Lord, I have hoped in you; let me never be put to shame.
In your righteousness deliver me and rescue me.   [Ps 70:1-2]

(And the rest of the passage.)

.3 And Isaiah says,

48   Pseudo-Epiphanius

47.3-51

[a.] Ἐπὶ τίνα ἀνοίξατε τὸ στόμα ὑμῶν; καὶ ἐπὶ τίνα
      ἐχαλάσατε τὴν γλῶσσαν ὑμῶν;

[b.] Ἀλλ' ἢ ἐπὶ τὸν πρᾷον καὶ ταπεινὸν καὶ ἡσύχιον.

[.4] Καὶ πάλιν·
      Ἐγενήθη ἡ κληρονομία μου ἐμοὶ ὡς λέων ἐν δρυμῷ·
      ἔδωκεν ἐπ' ἐμὲ φωνὴν αὐτῆς, διὰ τοῦτο ἐμίσησα
      αὐτήν. οὐκ ἐγὼ παρῃτησάμην ἀλλ' αὐτοὶ
      παρῃτήσαντό με. διὰ τοῦτο ἐγκαταλέλιπα τὸν
      οἶκόν μου.

[48] μη ὅτι ῥαπίσουσιν αὐτὸν καὶ ἐξουθενήσουσιν--

[.1] Μιχαιας λέγει·
      Πατάξουσιν ἐπὶ σιαγόνα τὸν κριτὴν τοῦ Ισραηλ.

[.2] Καὶ·
      Βδελυσσόμενον ὑπὸ τῶν ἐθνῶν τῶν δούλων τῶν
      ἀρχόντων· βασιλεῖς ὄψονται αὐτὸν καὶ ἀναστήσονται
      ἄρχοντες καὶ προσκυνήσουσιν αὐτόν.

[.3] Καὶ ἀλλαχοῦ λέγει·
      Ἐγὼ δὲ οὐκ ἀπειθῶ οὐδὲ ἀντιλέγω. τὸν νῶτόν μου
      δέδωκα εἰς μάστιγας, τὰς δὲ σιαγόνας μου εἰς
      ῥαπίσματα, τὸ δὲ πρόσωπόν μου οὐκ ἀπέστρεψα ἀπὸ
      αἰσχύνης ἐμπτυσμάτων.

[49] μθ ὅτι φεύξονται οἱ ἀπόστολοι--

[.1] Δαυιδ ἐν τῷ λζ ψαλμῷ λέγει·
      Οἱ φίλοι μου καὶ οἱ πλησίον μου ἐξ ἐναντίας μου
      ἤγγισαν καὶ ἔστησαν.

[.2] Καὶ πάλιν·
      Ἐμάκρυνας τοὺς γνωστούς μου ἀπ' ἐμοῦ.

[.3] Καὶ·
      Ἐζήτησα συλλυπούμενον, καὶ οὐκ ὑπῆρξε,
      καὶ παρακαλοῦντα, καὶ οὐκ εὗρον.

[50] ν ὅτι ἀρνήσεται Πετρος--

      Ησαιας λέγει·
      Καὶ ἐφοβήθη ἀπὸ ἀνθρώπου θνητοῦ, οἳ ὡσεὶ χόρτος
      ἀποξηρανθήσονται· ἐμοῦ δὲ ἐπελάθετο, λέγει Κύριος.

[51] να ὅτι σταυρώσουσιν αὐτόν--

47.4 παρῃτησαμην] παραιτησαμην 28, 790. / παρῃτησαντο] παραιτησαντο 28.
48.3 απεστρεψα] απεστραφη 790. / εμπτυσματων] εμπτυσμετων 28,
      επτυσματων 790.
49.1 οι φιλοι...παλιν] om 790.

a. Against whom will you open your mouth? And against whom
have you loosed your tongue?   [Isa 57:4]

b. But against the gentle and the humble and the meek. [Isa 66:2]

.4 And again,

My inheritance has come to me as a lion in a forest. It
has raised its voice against me. Therefore I have hated
it. I did not refuse, but they rejected me. Therefore
I have abandoned my house.   [Jer 12:7-8; unknown source]

48 That they would strike him and despise him--

.1 Micah says,

They will strike the judge of Israel on the cheek. [Mic 4:14]

.2 And [Isaiah says],

He is abhorred by the Gentiles, the servants of rulers.
Kings will see him and rulers will rise and will worship
him.   [Isa 49:7]

.3 And elsewhere he says,

I do not disobey or dispute. I give my back to scourges
and my cheeks to blows, and I have not turned my face away
from the shame of being spat upon.   [Isa 50:5-7]

49 That the apostles would flee--

.1 In the 37th Psalm, David says,

My friends and my neighbors drew near and took their stand
opposite me.   [Ps 37:12]

.2 And again,

You have removed my friends from me.   [Ps 87:9]

.3 And [again],

I looked for someone to grieve with, and there was none,
and someone to comfort, but I found none.   [Ps 68:21]

50 That Peter would deny him--

Isaiah says,

And he was afraid of mortal man, those who will be dried up
like grass; and he has forgotten me, says the Lord.
                                        [Isa 51:12-13; Ps 36:2]

51 That they would cruficy him--

51.1-54

[.1]   Ιερεμιας λέγει·
         'Εγὼ δὲ ὡς ἀρνίον ἄκακον ἀγόμενον τοῦ θύεσθαι.

[.2]   Καὶ Ησαΐας λέγει·
         'Ὡς πρόβατον ἐπὶ σφραγὴν ἤχθη καὶ ὡς ἀμνὸς
         ἐναντίον τοῦ κείροντος αὐτὸν ἄφωνος.

[.3]   Καὶ ἡ Σοφία λέγει·
         Θανάτῳ ἀσχήμονι καταδικάσωμεν αὐτόν.

[.4]   Καὶ πάλιν·
         Δεῦτε καὶ ἐμβάλωμεν ξύλον εἰς τὸν ἄρτον αὐτοῦ
         καὶ ἐκτρίψωμεν αὐτὸν ἐκ γῆς ζώντων.

[.5]   Καὶ Δαυιδ λέγει·
         "Ωρυξαν χεῖράς μου καὶ πόδας μου.

[52] $\overline{νβ}$ ὅτι ἀκάνθαις στεφανώσουσιν αὐτόν--

[.1]   'Εν τοῖς "Ασμασι λέγει·
         'Εξέλθετε καὶ ἴδετε, θυγατέρες Ιερουσαλημ,
         ἐν τῷ στεφάνῳ ᾧ ἐστεφάνωσεν αὐτὸν ἡ μήτηρ αυτοῦ.

[.2]   Καὶ Ησαΐας λέγει·
         "Εμεινα τοῦ ποιῆσαι σταφυλήν, ἐποίησε δέ ἀκάνθας.

[53] $\overline{νγ}$ ὅτι ὄξος καὶ χολὴν ποτίσουσιν αὐτόν--

[.1]   Δαυιδ ἐν τῷ $\overline{ξη}$ ψαλμῷ λέγει·
         "Εδωκαν εἰς τὸ βρῶμά μου χολὴν
         και εἰς τὴν δίψαν μου ἐπότισάν με ὄξος.

[.2]   Καὶ Μωυσης λέγει·
         Ταῦτα Κυρίῳ ἀνταποδίδοτε;

[.3]   Καὶ ἐν τοῖς "Ασμασι λέγει·
         Εἰσῆλθεν εἰς τὸν κῆπόν μου, ἀδελφή μου, νύμφη μου·
         καὶ ἐτρύγησαν σμύρναν μου.

[.4]   Καὶ πάλιν·
         Χεῖρές μου ἔσταξαν σμύρναν,
         καὶ οἱ δάκτυλοι μου σμύρναν πλήρεις.

[.5]   Καὶ πάλιν λέγει·
         Ποτιῶ σε ἀπὸ τοῦ οἴνου τοῦ μυρεψικοῦ.

[54] $\overline{νδ}$ ὅτι κόκκινον ἱμάτιον ἐνδύσουσιν αὐτόν--

51.2 ηχθη] margin, different hand 28.
53.4 σμυρναν[2]] σμυρνης 790.
53.5 του[1]] om 790.

.1   Jeremiah says,

    But as an innocent lamb I was led to be sacrificed.

                                    [Jer 11:19]

.2   And Isaiah says,

    As a sheep he was led to slaughter, and as a lamb before
    its shearer he was dumb.   [Isa 53:7]

.3   And Wisdom says,

    Let us condemn him to a shameful death.   [Wis 2:20]

.4   And again,

    Come and let us put wood into his bread, and let us drive
    him out from the land of the living.   [Jer 11:19]

.5   And David says,

    They pierced my hands and my feet.   [Ps 21:17]

52   That they would crown him with thorns--

.1   In the [Song of] Songs it says,

    Go forth and behold him, daughters of Jerusalem,
    in the crown with which his mother crowned him.   [Cant 3:11]

.2   And Isaiah says,

    I waited for it to bring forth grapes, but it brought forth
    thorns.   [Isa 5:2]

53   That they would give him vinegar and gall to drink--

.1   In the 68th Psalm, David says,

    They gave [me] gall for my food
    and gave me vinegar to drink for my thirst.   [Ps 68:22]

.2   And Moses says,

    Do you repay this to the Lord?   [Deut 32:6]

.3   And in the [Song of] Songs it says,

    She came into my garden, my sister, my spouse,
    and I gathered my myrrh.   [Cant 5:1]

.4   And again,

    My hands were dripping myrrh,
    and my fingers were full of myrrh.   [Cant 5:5]

.5   And again it says,

    I would make you drink from spiced wine.   [Cant 8:2]

54   That they would put a scarlet robe on him--

Ησαΐας λέγει·

Τίς οὗτος ὁ παραγενόμενος ἐξ Εδωμ, ἐρύθημα ἱμάτια
αὐτοῦ ἐκ Βοσορ, οὗτος ὡραῖος ἐν στολῇ αὐτοῦ βία;
ἵνα τί σου ἐρυθρὰ τὰ ἱμάτια καὶ τὰ ἐνδύματά σου
ὡς ἀπὸ πατητοῦ ληνοῦ;

[55] νε ὅτι σιωπήσει κρινόμενος--

[.1] Δαυιδ ἐν τῷ λζ ψαλμῷ λέγει·

Ἐγενόμην ὡσεὶ ἄνθρωπος οὐκ ἀκούων
καὶ οὐκ ἔχων ἐν τῷ στόματι αὐτοῦ ἐλεγμούς.

[.2] Καὶ πάλιν·

Ἐγὼ δὲ ὡσεὶ κωφὸς οὐκ ἤκουον
καὶ ὡσει ἄλαλος οὐκ ἀνοίγων τὸ στόμα αὐτοῦ.

[.3] Καὶ Ησαΐας λέγει·

Καὶ αὐτὸς διὰ τὸ κεκακοῖσθαι αὐτὸν οὐκ ἀνοίγει τὸ
στόμα αὐτοῦ· ὡς πρόβατον ἐπὶ σφαγὴν ἤχθη καὶ ὡς
ἀμνὸς ἐναντίον τοῦ κείροντος αὐτὸν ἄφωνος οὕτως
οὐκ ἀνοίγη τὸ στόμα αὐτοῦ ἐν τῇ ταπεινώσει.

[56] νς ὅτι χλευαστήσεται--

[.1] Δαυιδ ἐν τῷ ρη ψαλμῷ λέγει·

Εἴδοσάν με, ἐσάλευσαν κεφαλὰς αὐτῶν.

[.2] Καὶ ἐν τῇ Σοφιᾳ λέγει·

[a.] Εἰ ἐστι δίκαιος υἱὸς θεοῦ, ἀντιλήψεται αὐτοῦ.

[b.] Ἐπαγγέλλεται γνῶσιν ἔχειν θεοῦ
καὶ παιδίον Κυρίου ἑαυτὸν ὀνομάζει.

[57] νζ ὅτι. αὐτός ἐστιν ἡ ζωὴ ὁ κρεμμάμενος ἐπὶ ξύλου--

[.1] Μωυσης λέγει·

Ἔσται ἡ ζωή σου κρεμμαμένη ἐπὶ ξύλου ἀπέναντι τῶν
ὀφθαλμῶν σου, καὶ φοβηθήσῃ ἡμέρας καὶ νυκτὸς καὶ
οὐ πιστεύσῃ τῇ ζωῇ σου.

[.2] Καὶ πάλιν λέγει·

Ἐπικατάρατος πᾶς ὁ κρεμμάμενος ἐπὶ ξύλου.

[58] νη ὅτι ἀπάθεια τὸ πάθος αὐτοῦ--

---

54   Βοσορ] Βοσωρ 28.
55.3 κεκακοισθαι] κεκακοισθε 790. / ανοιγει] ανοιγη 790. / εν τη
      ταπεινωσει] om 790.
56.2b επαγγελλεται] επαγγελεται 790.
57.1 εσται] εσται φησιν 28. / κρεμμαμενη] κρεμαμενη 790.
57.2 κρεμμαμενος] κρεμαμενος 790.

Isaiah says,

Who is this who comes from Edom, his garments made red from
Bosor, this fair one, the man mighty in his raiment? Why are
your garments red, and your clothing as if from treading
a winepress?   [Isa 63:1-2]

55 That he would be silent while being judged--

.1 In the 37th Psalm, David says,

I became as a man who does not hear
and who does not have any reproofs in his mouth.   [Ps 37:15]

.2 And again,

And like a deaf man I did not hear,
and like a dumb man not opening his mouth.   [Ps 37:14]

.3 And Isaiah says,

And he, throughout his affliction, does not open his mouth;
he was led as a sheep to the slaughter, and as a lamb before
its shearer is dumb, so he does not open his mouth while
he is being humiliated.   [Isa 53:7]

56 That he would be mocked--

.1 In the 108th Psalm, David says,

They saw me; they shook their heads.   [Ps 108:25]

.2 And in Wisdom, it says,

a. If the just man is God's son, he will help him.   [Wis 2:18]

b. He claims to have knowledge of God,
   and he calls himself a child of the Lord.   [Wis 2:13]

57 That he is the life which hangs on the wooden stake--

.1 Moses says,

Your life will be hanging on a wooden stake before your eyes,
and you will be afraid day and night, and you will have no
confidence in your life.   [Deut 28:66]

.2 And again he says,

Cursed be everyone who hangs on a wooden stake.
                                        [Deut 21:23; Gal 3:13]

58 That his passion would be passionless--

[.1]   Ησαΐας βοᾷ λέγων·

            Ἡμεῖς ἐλογισάμεθα αὐτὸν εἶναι ἐν πόνῳ καὶ ἐν
            πληγῇ· αὐτὸς δὲ ἐτραυματίσθη διὰ τὰς ἀνομίας
            ἡμῶν καὶ μεμαλάκισται διὰ τὰς ἁμαρτίας ἡμῶν·
            παιδεία εἰρήνης ἡμῶν ἐπ' αὐτόν, καὶ τῷ μώλωπι
            αὐτοῦ ἡμεῖς οἱ πάντες ἰάθημεν.

[.2]   Καὶ ὁ Σιραχ λέγει·

            Ἔτυπτόν με, καὶ οὐκ ἐπόνεσα.

[.3]   Καὶ Δαυιδ ἐν τῷ ξ̅γ̅ ψαλμῷ λέγει·

            Βέλος νηπίων ἐγενήθησαν αἱ πληγαὶ αὐτῶν.

[59]   ν̅θ̅ ὅτι ἐν νυκτί, ψύζους ὄντος καὶ ἀνθρακιᾶς κειμένης, παθῇ
        ὁ Χριστός--

            Ζαχαριας λέγει·

            Καὶ ἔσται ἐν ἐκείνῃ τῇ ἡμέρᾳ ψῦχος, καὶ πάγος μίαν
            ἡμέραν ἔσται.

[60]   ξ̅ ὅτι δύσεται ὁ ἥλιος--

[.1]   Ζαχαριας πρώτως λέγει·

            Καὶ ἔσται ἐν ἐκείνῃ τῇ ἡμέρᾳ οὐκ ἔσται φῶς· καὶ
            ἡ ἡμέρα ἐκείνη γνωστὴ τῷ Κυρίῳ, καὶ οὐκ ἡμέρα
            οὐδὲ νύξ, καὶ πρὸς ἑσπέραν ἔσται φῶς.

[.2]   Καὶ Ιωηλ λέγει·

            Πρὸ προσώπου αὐτοῦ συναχθήσεται ἡ γῆ καὶ σκοτισ-
            θήσεται ὁ οὐρανός· ἥλιος καὶ σελήνη συσκοτάσουσι
            καὶ τὰ ἄστρα δύσουσι τὸ φέγγος αὐτῶν.

[61]   ξ̅α̅ ὅτι δύσεται ὁ ἥλιος μεσημβρίας--

            Αμως λέγει·

            Καὶ ἔσται ἐν ἐκείνῃ τῇ ἡμέρᾳ, λέγει Κύριος ὁ
            θεός, δύσεται ὁ ἥλιος μεσημβρίας, καὶ συσκοτάσει
            ἐπὶ γῆς ἐν ἡμέρᾳ τὸ φῶς αὐτοῦ, καὶ μεταστρέφει
            τὰς ἑορτὰς ἡμῶν εἰς πένθος.

[62]   ξ̅β̅ ὅτι τὰ ἱμάτια αὐτοῦ διαμερισόνται--

            Δαυιδ ἐν τῷ ξ̅α̅ ψαλμῷ λέγει·

            Διαμερίσαντο τὰ ἱμάτιά μου ἑαυτοῖς
            καὶ ἐπὶ τὸν ἱματισμόν μου ἔβαλον κλῆρον.

58.1   βοα λεγων] λεγει 790./ ειναι] om 28. / ανομιας...τας²] om 790. /
        οι] om 28.
59   παθη] παθοι 28, 790.
60.1   πρωτως] om 790.
61   ο¹] om 790.
62   διαμερισαντο] διεμερισαντο 28. / μου²] om 28.

.1 Isaiah cries out, saying,

We supposed him to be subject to trouble and stripes, but he
was wounded on account of our lawless deeds and weakened on
account of our iniquities. The chastisement that brought
peace to us came upon him, and by his bruises we were all
healed.   [Isa 53:4-5]

.2 And Sirach says,

They struck me, and I did not know it.   [Prov 23:35]

.3 And in the 63rd Psalm, David says,

Their blows became a children's arrow.   [Ps 63:8]

59 That in the night, when it was cold and there was a charcoal
fire, the Christ would suffer--

Zechariah says,

And it will be cold in that day, and there will be frost for
one day.   [Zech 14:6-7]

60 That the sun would set--

.1 First, Zechariah says,

And it will be in that day that there will be no light; and
that day will be known to the Lord, and will be neither day
nor night, and towards evening it will be light. [Zech 14:6-7]

.2 And Joel says,

Before his face the earth will be drawn together and heaven
will be darkened; the sun and moon will grow dark, and the
stars will withdraw their light.   [Joel 2:10]

61 That the sun would set at midday--

Amos says,

And it will be in that day, says the Lord God, that the sun
will set at midday, and its light will be darkened on the
earth in the day, and it will turn our feasts into mourning.
                                                 [Amos 8:9-10]

62 That his garments would be divided--

In the 21st Psalm, David says,

They divided my clothing among themselves
and over my garment they cast lots.   [Ps 21:19]

[63]　ξγ̄　ὅτι συσταυρωθήσεται λησταῖς--

Ἠσαΐας λέγει·

Καὶ μετὰ ἀνόμων ἐλογίσθη, καὶ παρεδώθη εἰς
θάνατον ἡ ψυχὴ αὐτοῦ.

[64]　ξδ̄　ὅτι τὴν πλευρὰν αὐτοῦ ἐκκεντήσουσιν--

Ζαχαριας λέγει·

"Οφονται εἰς ὃν ἐξεκέντησαν.

[65]　ξε̄　ὅτι ὀστοῦν αὐτοῦ οὐ συντριβήσεται--

Μυωσης λέγει·

'Οστοῦν οὐ συντριβήσεται ἀπ' αὐτοῦ.

[66]　ξϛ̄　ὅτι ἐκ τῆς πλευρὰς αὐτοῦ ὕδωρ ῥυήσεται εἰς βαπτίσματος
τύπον--

Ἠσαΐας λέγει·

"Αρτος αὐτῷ δοθήσεται, καὶ τὸ ὕδωρ αὐτοῦ πιστόν.

[67]　ξζ̄　ὅτι ἐν πέτρᾳ τεθήσεται--

Ἠσαΐας λέγει·

'Εμβλέψατε εἰς τὴν στερεὰν πέτραν, ἣν ἐλατομήσατε,
καὶ εἰς τὸν βόθυνον τοῦ λάκκου, ὃν ὠρύξατε.

[68]　ξη̄　ὅτι λίθος ἡ θύρα τοῦ μνήματος--

'Ο αὐτὸς λέγει·

Καὶ ἐπέθηκαν λίθον ἐπ' ἐμε.

[69]　ξθ̄　ὅτι σφραγίσουσιν--

Δανιηλ λέγει·

Καὶ ἤνεγκαν λίθον ἕνα καὶ ἐπέθηκαν ἐπὶ τὸ στόμα
τοῦ λάκκου, καὶ ἐσφραγίσατο ὁ βασιλεὺς ἐν τῷ
δακτυλίῳ αὐτοῦ καὶ ἐν τῷ δακτυλίῳ τῶν μεγιστάνων
αὐτοῦ, ὅπως μὴ ἀλλοιωθῇ πρᾶγμα ἐν τῷ Δανιηλ.

[70]　ō　ὅτι θέρους ἀρχομένου ἔσται τὸ πάθος αὐτοῦ, μηνὶ τῷ καθ'
ἡμᾶς Μαρτίῳ--

'Εν τοῖς "Ἀσμασι λέγει·

'Ο καιρὸς παρῆλθεν·
ἐπορεύθη ἑαυτῷ τὰ ἔθνη·
ὤφθη ἐν τῇ γῇ,
καιρὸς τῆς τομῆς ἔφθασεν.

64　την πλευραν] των πλευρην 28.
66　τυπον] τυπονι 790.
70　θερους] θερος 28. / εθνη] εμθη 28. / εφθασεν] πεφθακεν 28.

63 That he would be crucified with insurgents--

Isaiah says,

And he was numbered with lawless ones, and his soul was
delivered to death.   [Isa 53:12]

64 That they would pierce his side--

Zecharaiah says,

They will look on the one whom they have pierced.
[Zech 12:10 (Heb); John 19:37]

65 That a bone of his would not be broken--

Moses says,

A bone of his will not be broken.   [Num 9:12]

66 That from his side water would flow (as a type indicating
baptizing)--

Isaiah says,

Bread will be given him, and his water is faithful.
[Isa 33:16]

67 That he would be placed in a rock--

Isaiah says,

Look to the solid rock which you have hewn, and to the hole
of the pit which you have dug.   [Isa 51:1]

68 That the door of the tomb would be a stone--

The same one says,

And they laid a stone on me.   [Lam 3:53]

69 That they would seal [the tomb]--

Daniel says,

And they brought one stone, and put it on the mouth of the
pit, and the king sealed it with his ring and with the ring
of his nobles, that the sentence might not be altered
concerning Daniel.   [Dan 6:18 (Th)]

70 That his suffering would be at the beginning of summer, in the
month which we call March--

In the [Song of] Songs, it says,

The time is passed;
the nations went from him;
he is seen in the land,
the harvest time has arrived.   [Cant 2:11-12]

[71]   οα ὅτι ταφήσεται--

[.1]   Ησαΐας λέγει·
          'Απὸ προσώπου ἀδικίας ἤρτηται ὁ δίκαιος· ἔσται ἐν
          εἰρήνῃ ἡ ταφὴ αὐτοῦ.

[.2]   Καὶ πάλιν λέγει·
          'Απὸ τῶν ἁμαρτιῶν τοῦ λαοῦ μου ἤχθη εἰς θάνατον·
          καὶ δώσω τοὺς πονηροὺς ἀντὶ τῆς ταφῆς αὐτοῦ καὶ
          τοὺς πλουσίους ἀντὶ τοῦ θανάτου αὐτοῦ.

[.3]   Καὶ Ιακωβ λέγει·
          'Αναπεσὼν ἐκοιμήθη ὡς λέων
          καὶ ὡς σκύμνος· τίς ἐγερεῖ αὐτόν;

[.4]   Καὶ ἐν τοῖς Αριθμοῖς λέγει·
          'Ανακλιθεὶς ἀνεπαύσατα ὡς λέων καὶ ὡς σκύμνος.

[.5]   Καὶ Δαυιδ ἐν τῷ κα ψαλμῷ λέγει·
          Εἰς χοῦν θανάτου κατήγαγές με.

[72]   οβ ὅτι φοβήσει τὸν Ἅδην ταφείς--

[.1]   'Εν τῷ ιωβ λέγει·
          'Ανοιχθήσονται αὐτῷ φόβῳ πύλαι θανάτου,
          πυλωροὶ δὲ τοῦ Ἅδου ἰδόντες σε ἔπτυξαν.

[.2]   Καὶ Ησαΐας λέγει·
          Ὁ Ἅδης ἐπικράνθη συναντήσας σοι κάτω.

[.3]   Καὶ Δαυιδ ἐν τῷ ρς ψαλμῷ λέγει·
          Συνέτριψε πύλας χαλκᾶς
          καὶ μοχλοὺς σιδηροῦς συνέθλασεν.

[73]   ογ ὅτι ἀναμάρτητος--

[.1]   Ησαΐας λέγει·
          Ὃς ἁμαρτίαν οὐκ ἐποίησεν, οὐδὲ εὑρέθη δόλος ἐν τῷ
          στόματι αὐτοῦ.

[.2]   Καὶ πάλιν·
          'Απὸ τῶν ἁμαρτιῶν τοῦ λαοῦ μου ἤχθη εἰς θάνατον.

[74]   οδ ὅτι ἀναστήσεται--

71.2 του²] om 790.
72.1 σε επτυξαν] αυτον εδειλιασαν 28.
72.2 επικρανθη...κατω] κατω επικρανθη συναντησας σοι 28.
73   αναμαρτητος] + erasure 28.

71   That he would be buried--

.1   Isaiah says,

The righteous one has been bound because of the presence of
unrighteousness. His burial will be in peace.   [Isa 57:1-2]

.2   And again he says,

Because of the sins of my people he was led to death; and I
will give the wicked in place of his burial, and the rich
in place of his death.   [Isa 53:8-9]

.3   And Jacob says,

Having lain down, he slept as a lion
and as a young lion. Who will raise him up?   [Gen 49:9]

.4   And in Numbers, it says,

He reclined, resting as a lion and as a young lion. [Num 24:9]

.5   And in the 21st Psalm, David says,

You have brought me down into the dust of death.   [Ps 21:16]

72   That his being buried would terrify Hades--

.1   In Job, it says,

The gates of death will open to him in fear,
and the porters of Hades cowered for fear when they saw you.
                                                  [Job 38:17]

.2   And Isaiah says,

Hades is stirred up in meeting you below.   [Isa 14:9]

.3   And in the 106th Psalm, David says,

He broke the brazen gates to pieces
and crushed the iron bars.   [Ps 106:16]

73   That he would be without sin--

.1   Isaiah says,

He committed no sin, nor was deceit found in his mouth.
                                                   [Isa 53:9]

.2   And again,

Because of the sins of my people, he was led to death.
                                                   [Isa 53:8]

74   That he would be raised up--

[.1]   Δαυιδ ἐν τῷ ι̅α̅ ψαλμῷ λέγει·

        "Ενεκεν τῆς ταλαιπωρίας τῶν πτωχῶν
        καὶ τοῦ στεναγμοῦ τῶν πενήτων
        νῦν ἀναστήσομαι, λέγει Κύριος.

[.2]   Καὶ πάλιν ὁ αὐτὸς λέγει ἐν τῷ ι̅ε̅ ψαλμῷ·

        "Οτι οὐκ ἐγκαταλείψεις τὴν ψυχήν μου εἰς "Ἀδην
        οὐδὲ δώσεις τὸν ὅσιόν σου ἰδεῖν διαφθοράν.

[.3]   Καὶ πάλιν ὁ αὐτὸς λέγει ἐν τῷ κ̅θ̅ ψαλμῷ·

        Ἀνήγαγες ἐξ "Ἀδου τὴν ψυχήν μου
        ἀπὸ τῶν καταβαινόντων εἰς λάκκον.

[.4]   Καὶ Ιερεμιας λέγει·

        Διὰ τοῦτο ἐξηγέρθην, καὶ ἰδοὺ καὶ ὁ ὕπνος μου ἡδὺς
        ἐγένετο.

[.5]   Καὶ Δαυιδ ἐν τῷ π̅ϛ̅ ψαλμῷ λέγει·

        Ἡμέρας ἐκέκραξα καὶ ἐν νυκτὶ ἐναντίον σου·
        προσελογίσθην μετὰ τῶν καταβαινόντων εἰς λάκκον.

[.6]   Καὶ πάλιν·

        Ἐγενήθην ὡσεὶ ἄνθρωπος ἀβοήθητος ἐν νεκροῖς
        ἐλεύθερος.

[.7]   Καὶ πάλιν ὁ αὐτὸς ἐν τῷ π̅α̅ ψαλμῷ λέγει·

        Ἀνάστα, ὁ θεὸς, κρίνων τὴν γῆν.

[.8]   Καὶ Ησαΐας λέγει·

        Ὁ ἀναγαγὼν ἐκ γῆς τὸν ποιμένα τῶν προβάτων τὸν
        μέγαν.

[.9]   Καὶ Ναουμ λέγει·

        Ταχεῖς ἰδοὺ οἱ πόδες ἐπὶ τὰ ὄρη εὐαγγελιζομένου
        εἰρήνην.

[75]   ο̅ε̅ ὅτι μάτην οἱ στρατιῶται τὸν τάφον τηρήσουσιν--

        Δαυιδ ἐν τῷ ο̅ε̅ ψαλμῷ λέγει·

        "Υπνωσαν ὕπνον αὐτῶν καὶ οὐκ εὗρον οὐδέν.

[76]   ο̅ϛ̅ ὅτι πρωὶ ἡ ἀνάστασις--

[.1]   Δαυιδ ἐν τῷ κ̅θ̅ ψαλμῷ λέγει·

        Τὸ ἑστέρας αὐλισθήσεται κλαυθμὸς
        καὶ εἰς τὸ πρωὶ ἀγαλλίασις.

74.1 αναστησομαι] αναστησομε 28, 790.
74.2 ψαλμω] ψαλμω λεγει 28.
74.3 λεγει] om 28. / ψαλμω] ψαλμω λεγει 28.
74.5 εν²] om 790./ λακκον] λακον 790.
75   αυτων] αυτην 28, αυτον 790.

.1 In the 11th Psalm, David says,

Because of the misery of the poor
and the sighs of the needy,
I will be raised up now, says the Lord.   [Ps 11:6]

.2 And again in the 15th Psalm, the same one says,

You will not leave my soul in Hades,
nor will you let your holy one see corruption.   [Ps 15:10]

.3 And in the 29th Psalm, the same one says,

You have brought up my soul from Hades,
from those who go down to the pit.   [Ps 29:4]

.4 And Jeremiah says,

Therefore I was awakened, and behold even my sleep became
sweet.   [Jer 38:26]

.5 And in the 87th Psalm, David says,

I have cried day and night before you;
I have been reckoned with those who go down to the pit.
                                                 [Ps 87:2, 5]

.6 And again,

I became like a helpless man, free among the dead.   [Ps 87:5]

.7 And again in the 81st Psalm, the same one says,

Arise, God, to judge the earth.   [Ps 81:8]

.8 And Isaiah says,

Who brought again from the earth the great shepherd of the
sheep.   [Isa 63:11; Heb 13:20]

.9 And Nahum says,

Behold, swift are the feet on the mountains of the one who
is proclaiming peace.   [Nah 1:14-2:1]

75 That the soldiers would guard the tomb in vain--

In the 75th Psalm, David says,

They have slept their sleep and not found anything.   [Ps 75:6]

76 That the resurrection would be in the early morning--

.1 In the 29th Psalm, David says,

Weeping will tarry for the evening
and rejoicing until the early morning.   [Ps 29:6]

76.2-81.2

[.2]   Καὶ πάλιν ἐν τῷ π̅ς̅ λέγει·

            Ἐγὼ πρὸς σέ, Κύριε, ἐκέκραξα,
            καὶ τὸ πρωὶ ἡ προσευχή μου προφθάσει σε.

[.3]   Καὶ πάλιν ἐν τῷ ν̅ς̅ λέγει·

            Ἐξεγέρθητι ψαλτήριον καὶ κιθάρα·
            ἐξεγερθήσομαι ὄρθρου.

[77]   ο̅ς̅ ὅτι μαρτύριον ὁ τόπος ἔσται--

            Ναουμ λέγει·

            Ἑτοιμάζου ὄρθρισον, διέφθαρται πᾶσα ἡ ὑποφυλλὶς
            αὐτῶν· διὰ τοῦτο ὑπόμεινόν με, λέγει Κύριος, εἰς
            ἡμέραν ἀναστάσεώς μου εἰς μαρτύριόν μου· διότι
            τὸ κρίμα μου ἄξει πάντας τοὺς ἐχθρούς μου.

[78]   ο̅η̅ ὅτι ἀπὸ τοῦ προτειχίσματος--

            Ἐν τοῖς Ἄσμασι λέγει·

            Ἀνάστα, ἐλθέ, ἡ πλησίον μου,
            ἐν σκέπῃ τῆς πέτρας,
            ἐχόμενα τοῦ προτειχίσματος.

[79]   ο̅θ̅ ὅτι ζητηθήσεται ὑπὸ γυναικῶν--

            Ἐν τοῖς Ἄσμασι λέγει·

            Ἐπὶ κοίτην μου
            ἐξεζήτησα ὃν ἠγάπησεν ἡ ψυχή μου,
            ἐζήτησα, καὶ οὐκ εὗρον αὐτόν.
            μὴ ὃν ἠγάπησεν ἡ ψυχή μου ἴδετε;

[80]   π̅   ὅτι πρῶτον ἀπαντήσει γυναιξί--

            Ἐν τοῖς Ἄσμασι λέγει·

            Εὗρον ὃν ἠγάπησεν ἡ ψυχή μου,
            ἐκράτησα αὐτὸν καὶ οὐκ ἀφῆκα αὐτόν.

[81]   π̅α̅ ὅτι ἀναχωρήσουσιν ἔμφοβοι--

[.1]   Δαυιδ ἐν τῷ β̅ ψαλμῷ λέγει·

            Δουλεύσατε τῷ Κυρίῳ ἐν φόβῳ
            καὶ ἀγαλλιᾶσθε αὐτῷ ἐν τρόμῳ.

[.2]   Καὶ Ἡσαΐας λέγει·

            Γυναῖκες ἐρχόμεναι ἀπὸ θέας, δεῦτε· οὐ γὰρ λαός
            ἐστιν ἔχων φρόνησιν.

76.2   προς σε Κυριε] Κυριε προς σε 28.
77   ορθρισον] ωσθρισον 28. / υποφυλλις] υποφυλις 28, 790.
78   η] om 28.
80   γυναιξι] γυνατοις 28.

.2 And again in the 87th, he says,

    I cried to you, Lord,
    and in the early morning my prayer will go before you.
                                             [Ps 87:14]

.3 And again in the 56th, he says,

    Awake, psaltery and harp;
    I will awake early.   [Ps 56:9]

77 That the place would be a witness--

    Nahum says,

    Prepare, rise early; all their produce is spoiled. Therefore
    wait for me, says the Lord, until the day of my rising, in
    order to bear witness to me, because my judgment will take
    away all my enemies.   [Zeph 3:7-8]

78 That [the resurrection would be] from inside the wall--

    In the [Song of] Songs, it says,

    Rise up, come, my companion
    in the shelter of the rock,
    you who are close by the wall.   [Cant 2:13-14]

79 That he would be sought by women--

    In the [Song of] Songs, it says,

    On my bed
    I sought out him whom my soul loves;
    I sought and did not find him.
    Have you seen him whom my soul loves?   [Cant 3:1, 3]

80 That he would meet women first--

    In the [Song of] Songs, it says,

    I found him whom my soul loves;
    I held him and did not let him go.   [Cant 3:4]

81 That they would run away terrified--

.1 In the 2d Psalm, David says,

    Serve the Lord with fear
    and rejoice in him with trembling.   [Ps 2:11]

.2 And Isaiah says,

    Come, women, come from seeing;
    for the people do not have understanding.   [Isa 27:11]

[82] π̅β̅ ὅτι ἐμφυσήσει τοῖς ἀποστόλοις τὸ πνεῦμα τὸ ἅγιον--

Ναουμ λέγει·

'Ετοιμάζου ὄρθρισον, διέφθαρται πᾶσα ἡ ὑποφυλλὶς
αὐτῶν. ἀνέβη γὰρ ἐμφυσιῶν εἰς τὸ πρόσωπον αὐτῶν.

[83] π̅γ̅ ὅτι ἀπὸ μέλιτος κηρίου φάγεται μετὰ τὴν ἀνάστασιν--

'Εν τοῖς "Ασμασι λέγει·

"Εφαγον ἄρτον μου μετὰ μέλιτός μου.

Τὸ πικρὸν πρὸ τοῦ πάθους, καὶ τὸ γλυκὺ μετὰ τὴν
ἀνάστασιν.

[84] π̅δ̅ ὅτι ἐροῦσιν ὅτι ἐκλάπη--

[.1]   Ιωνας λέγει·

Φυλασσόμενοι μάταια καὶ ψευδῆ ἔλεον αὐτῶν
ἐγκατέλιπον.

[.2]   Καὶ Ησαΐας λέγει·

'Αλλὰ λέγετε ἡμῖν καὶ ἀπαγγέλλετε ἡμῖν ἑτέραν
πλάνησιν.

[85] π̅ε̅ ὅτι νεκροὶ ἀναστήσονται--

[.1]   Ωσηε λέγει·

'Ορθριοῦσι πρός με λέγοντες· πορευθῶμεν καὶ
ἐπιστρέψωμεν πρὸς Κύριον, ὅτι αὐτὸς πέπαικε καὶ
ἰάσεται ἡμᾶς, πατάξει καὶ ὑγιάσει ἡμᾶς μετὰ δύο
ἡμέρας, καὶ ἐν τῇ ἡμέρᾳ τῇ τρίτῃ ἀναστησόμεθα
ἐναντίον αὐτοῦ.

[.2]   Καὶ Ησαΐας λέγει·

'Αναστήσονται οἱ νεκροί, καὶ ἐγερθήσονται οἱ ἐν
τοῖς μνημείοις, καὶ εὐφρανθήσονται οἱ ἐν τῇ γῇ.

[.3]   Καὶ Ζαχαριας λέγει·

Καὶ σὺ ἐν αἵματι διαθήκης ἐξαπέστειλας δεσμίους σου
ἐκ λάκκου οὐκ ἔχοντος ὕδωρ.

[.4]   Καὶ πάλιν Ωσηε λέγει·

'Εκ χειρὸς "Ἀδου ῥύσομαι αὐτοὺς, καὶ ἐκ θανάτου
λυτρώσομαι αὐτούς· ποῦ ἡ δίκη σου θάνατε; ποῦ
τὸ κέντρον σου "Ἀδη;

---

82   υποφυλλις] υποφυλις 28, 790.
84.1 ελεον] ελαιον 790.
84.2 ημιν] om 790. / απαγγελλετε] απαγγελλεται 790.
85.1 πεπαικε] πεπεκε 28, πεπωκε 790. / υγιασει] υγιωσει 790.
85.4 παλιν...λεγει] Ωσηε παλιν 790.

82 That he would breathe the Holy Spirit into the apostles--
Nahum says,

> Prepare, rise early; all their appearance is distorted. For
> he ascended breathing into their face.   [Zeph 3:7; Nah 2:2]

83 That after the resurrection he would eat from honey of the
honeycomb--

In the [Song of] Songs, it says,

> I have eaten my bread with my honey.   [Cant 5:1]

(The bitter comes before the suffering, and the sweet after
the resurrection.)

84 That they would say that [his body] was stolen--

.1 Jonah says,

> Those who repeat vain and false reports have forsaken their
> own mercy.   [Jonah 2:9]

.2 And Isaiah says,

> But speak to us and announce to us another deception.
> [Isa 30:10]

85 That the dead would be raised up--

.1 Hosea says,

> They will rise up to me early saying, Let us go and return
> to the Lord, for he has struck and will heal us; he will
> slay and cure us after two days, and in the third day we
> will be raised up in his presence.   [Hos 6:1-2]

.2 And Isaiah says,

> The dead will arise, and those who are in the tombs will be
> raised up, and those who are in the earth will rejoice.
> [Isa 26:19]

.3 And Zechariah says,

> And you in the blood of the covenant have sent forth your
> prisoners out of the pit that has no water.   [Zech 9:11]

.4 And again Hosea says,

> I will deliver them out of the hand of Hades, and will redeem
> them from death. Where is your judgment, death? Where is
> your sting, Hades?   [Hos 13:14]

[.5]   Καὶ Ιεζεκιηλ λέγει·

Τάδε λέγει Κύριος· ἀνοίγω τὰ μνήματα ὑμῶν καὶ ἀνάξω
ὑμᾶς ἐκ τῶν μνημάτων καὶ εἰσάξω ὑμᾶς εἰς τὴν γῆν
τοῦ Ισραηλ, καὶ γνώσεσθε ὅτι ἐγώ εἰμι Κύριος ἐν
τῷ ἀνοιξαί με τοὺς τάφους ὑμῶν τοῦ ἀναγαγεῖν με
ὑμᾶς ἐκ τῶν τάφων ὑμῶν λαός μου· καὶ δώσω πνεῦμα
εἰς ὑμᾶς, καὶ ζήσεσθε.

[86]   π̅ε̅ ὅτι εἰς οὐρανοὺς ἀνελεύσεται--

[.1]   Δαυιδ ἐν τῷ μ̅ε̅ ψαλμῷ λέγει·

Ἀνέβη ὁ θεὸς ἐν ἀλαλαγμῷ,
Κύριος ἐν φωνῇ σάλπιγγος.

[.2]   Καὶ Αμως λέγει·

Ὁ οἰκοδομῶν εἰς οὐρανὸν τὴν ἐπίβασιν αὐτοῦ.

[87]   π̅ζ̅ ὅτι αὐτὸς ἦν ὁ κηρύξας--

[.1]   Ησαιας λέγει·

Πνεῦμα Κυρίου ἐπ' ἐμέ, οὗ εἵνεκεν ἔχρισέ με·
εὐαγγελίσασθαι πτωχοῖς ἀπέσταλκέ με, κηρύξαι
αἰχμαλώτοις ἄφεσιν καὶ τυφλοῖς ἀνάβλεψιν, καλέσαι
ἐνιαυτὸν Κυρίῳ δεκτὸν καὶ ἡμέραν ἀνταποδώσεως
τῷ θεῷ ἡμῶν.

[.2]   Καὶ πάλιν·

Γνώσεται ὁ λαός μου τὸ ὄνομά μου ἐν τῇ ἡμέρᾳ
ἐκείνῃ, ὅτι ἐγώ εἰμι αὐτὸς ὁ λαλῶν· πάρειμι ὡς
ὡραῖος ἐπὶ τῶν ὡραίων, ὡς εὐαγγελιζόμενος ἀκοὴν
εἰρήνης, ἀκουστὴν ποιῶν τὴν σωτηρίαν σου.

[88]   π̅η̅ ὅτι ἐν πάσῃ τῇ γῇ τὸ ὄνομα αὐτοῦ--

[.1]   Ζαχαριας λέγει·

Καὶ ἔσται ὅσοι ἐὰν καταλειφθῶσιν ἐκ πάντων τῶν
ἐθνῶν τῶν ἐλθόντων ἐπὶ Ιερουσαλημ, ἀναβήσονται
κατ' ἐνιαυτὸν προσκυνῆσαι Κυρίῳ παντοκράτορι.

[.2]   Καὶ Ιεζεκιηλ λέγει·

Καθαριῶ ὑμᾶς, καὶ τὸ πνεῦμά μου δώσω ἐν ὑμῖν.

[.3]   Καὶ πάλιν·

Δώσω αὐτοῖς καρδίαν ἑτέραν καὶ πνεῦμα καινὸν δώσω
αὐτοῖς.

[.4]   Καὶ Δαυιδ ἐν τῷ ι̅η̅ ψαλμῷ λέγει·

Εἰς πᾶσαν τὴν γῆν ἐξῆλθεν ὁ φθόγγος αὐτοῦ
καὶ εἰς τὰ πέρατα τῆς οἰκουμένης τὰ ῥήματα αὐτοῦ.

85.5 Κυριος²] θεος 790.
87.1 εινεκεν] ενεκεν 28, ινεκεν 790.
87.2 ωραιος] ωραια 28. / ακοην] om 790. / ειρηνης] ειρηνην 790.
88.4 αυτου...αυτου] αυτων. και τα εξης 790.

.5   And Ezekiel says,

This is what the Lord says: I am opening your tombs and will
bring you out of your tombs and will bring you into the land
of Israel; and you will know that I am Lord when I open your
graves to bring you up from your graves as my people; and I
will give you breath, and you will live.   [Ezek 37:12-14]

86   That he would be taken up into heaven--

.1   In the 46th Psalm, David says,

God ascended with a shout,
the Lord with the sound of a trumpet.   [Ps 46:6]

.2   And Amos says,

He who builds his path to heaven.   [Amos 9:6]

87   That he was the herald--

Isaiah says,

The spirit of the Lord is upon me because he has anointed me.
He has sent me to preach news to the poor, to proclaim liberty
to the captives and recovery of sight to the blind, to
declare an acceptable year to the Lord and a day of
repayment to our God.   [Isa 61:1-2]

.2   And again,

My people will know my name in that day, for I am he who
speaks.   I am present as the fair among the fair, as the
proclaimer of tidings of peace, the publisher of your
salvation.   [Isa 52:6-7]

88   That his name [would be known] in the whole earth--

.1   Zechariah says,

And it will happen that whoever will be left from all the
nations that come against Jerusalem will come up every year
to worship the Lord almighty.   [Zech 14:16]

.2   And Ezekiel says,

I will cleanse you, and will put my spirit in you.
                                                     [Ezek 36:25, 27]

.3   And again,

I will give them another heart, and will give them a new
spirit.   [Ezek 36:26]

.4   And in the 18th Psalm, David says,

His voice is gone out into all the earth
and his words to the end of the inhabited earth.   [Ps 18:5]

[.5]   Καὶ Ιερεμιας λέγει·

           Δώσω αὐτοῖς ὁδὸν ἑτέραν καὶ καρδίαν ἑτέραν τοῦ
           φόβεισθαί με πάσας τὰς ἡμέρας.

[89]   π̄θ̄ ὅτι ἐκ δεξιῶν τοῦ Πατρὸς οὐκ ἀφ' οὗ ἀνῆλθεν ἐκάθισεν,
           ἀλλὰ καὶ πρὸ τούτου--

[.1]   Ησαΐας λέγει·

           Εἶδον τὸν Κύριον καθήμενον ἐπὶ θρόνου ὑψηλοῦ καὶ
           ἐπηρμένου.

[.2]   Καὶ Δαυιδ ἐν τῷ ϙ̄β̄ λέγει·

           "Ετοιμος ὁ θρόνος σου, Κύριε, καὶ ἀπὸ τότε,
           ἀπο τοῦ αἰῶνος συ εἶ.

[.3]   Καὶ πάλιν ἐν τῷ ρ̄θ̄ λέγει·

           Εἶπεν ὁ Κύριος τῷ Κυρίῳ μου· κάθου ἐκ δεξιῶν μου,
           ἕως ἂν θῶ τοὺς ἐχθρούς σου ὑποπόδιον τῶν ποδῶν σου.

[.4]   Καὶ Ησαΐας λέγει·

           'Ο οὐρανός μοι θρόνος, ἡ δὲ γῆ ὑποπόδιον τῶν ποδῶν
           μου.

[90]   ϙ̄ ὅτι κληθησόμεθα Χριστιανοί--

[.1]   Ησαΐας λέγει·

           "Οψονται ἔθνη τὴν δόξαν σου καὶ πάντες οἱ βασιλεῖς
           τὴν δικαιοσύνην σου, καὶ καλέσει σε τὸ ὄνομα τὸ
           καινόν, ὃ ὁ Κύριος ὀνομάσει αὐτῷ.

[.2]   Καὶ πάλιν·

           Τοῖς δὲ δουλεύουσί μοι κληθήσεται ὄνομα καινόν,
           ὃ εὐλογηθήσεται ἐπὶ τῆς γῆς.

[91]   ϙ̄ᾱ ὅτι καὶ ἡ ἐπὶ τοῦ μετώπου σημείωσις προκατηγγέλετο--

[.1]   Δαυιδ ἐν τῷ ν̄θ̄ ψαλμῷ λέγει·

           "Εδωκας τοῖς φοβουμένοις σε σημείωσιν
           τοῦ φυγεῖν ἀπὸ προσώπου τόξου.

[.2]   Καὶ Ησαΐας λέγει·

           Φανεροὶ ἔσονται οἱ σφραγιζόμενοι τὸν νόμον μαθεῖν.

[.3]   Καὶ Ιεζεκιηλ λέγει·

           Εἶπε Κύριος πρὸς τὸν ἄνδρα τὸν ἐνδεδυκότα τὸν
           ποδήρη, δὸς τὴν σημείωσιν ἐπὶ τὰ μέτωπα τῶν ἀνδρῶν
           τῶν καταστεναζόντων καὶ κατωδυνωμένων ἐπὶ πάσαις
           ταῖς ἀδικίαις, καὶ διέλθετε μέσην τὴν Ιερουσαλημ·

89.2 λεγει] λεγει ψαλμω 28. / κυριε και] om 790.
89.3 λεγει] λεγει ψαλμω 28.
91   επι] om 790. / προκατηγγελετο] προκατηγγελλετο 28.

.5 And Jeremiah says,

    I will give them another way and another heart, to fear me
    all their days.   ·   [Jer 39:39]

89 That he sat at the right hand of the father, not only after he
    ascended, but even before that--

.1 Isaiah says,

    I saw the Lord sitting on a high and exalted throne. [Isa 6:1]

.2 And in the 92d, David says,

    Your throne is prepared, Lord, even from that time;
    you are from eternity.   [Ps 92:2]

.3 And again in the 109th, he says,

    The Lord said to my Lord, Sit at my right hand
    until I make your enemies a footstool for your feet.
                                      [Ps 109:1]

.4 And Isaiah says,

    Heaven is my throne and earth is a footstool for my feet.
                                      [Isa 66:1]

90 That we would be called Christians--

.1 Isaiah says,

    Gentiles will see your glory and all the kings your
    righteousness, and he will give you a new name which the
    Lord will call you.   [Isa 62:2]

.2 And again,

    And my servants will be given a new name, which will be
    blessed on the earth.   [Isa 65:15-16]

91 That even the mark on the forehead was foretold--

.1 In the 59th Psalm, David says,

    You have placed a mark on those who fear you
    so that they might flee from the face of the bow.   [Ps 59:6]

.2 And Isaiah says,

    Those who seal themselves to learn the law will be made
    manifest.   [Isa 8:16]

.3 And Ezekiel says,

    The Lord said to the man clothed with the long robe, Put the
    mark on the foreheads of the men who groan and grieve over
    all the injustices, and go through the middle of Jerusalem

καὶ κόπτετε καὶ μὴ φείσησθε καὶ μὴ ἐλεήσητε·
πρεσβύτερον καὶ νεανίσκον καὶ γυναῖκας, νήπια
θηλάζοντα πάντας ἐξαλείψατε· ἐπὶ δὲ πάντας ἐφ'
οὓς ἐστι τὸ σημεῖόν μου μὴ ἐγγίσητε.

[92] ϙ̅β̅ ὅτι τὸ ἐν τῷ Χριστῷ βάπτισμα προκατηγγέλετο--

[.1]   Ἡσαΐας λέγει·

Λούσασθε, καθαροὶ γίνεσθε, ἀφέλετε τὰς πονηρίας
ὑμῶν ἀπὸ τῶν ψυχῶν ὑμῶν ἀπέναντι τῶν ὀφθαλμῶν μου.

[.2]   Καὶ πάλιν τρανώτερον·

Τῇ ἡμέρᾳ ἐκείνῃ ἐπιλάμψει ὁ θεὸς ἐν βουλῇ μετὰ
δόξης ἐπὶ τῆς γῆς τοῦ ὑψῶσαι καὶ δοξάσαι τὸ
καταληφθὲν τοῦ Ισραηλ ἐν Σιων, καὶ τὸ καταλειφθὲν
ἐν Ιερουσαλημ, ὅτι ἅγιοι κληθήσονται πάντες οἱ
γραφέντες εἰς ζωὴν ἐν Ιερουσαλημ· ὅτι ἐκπλυνεῖ
Κύριος τὸν ῥύπον τῶν υἱῶν καὶ τῶν θυγατέρων Σιων
καὶ τὸ αἷμα Ιερουσαλημ ἐκκαθαριεῖ ἐκ μέσου αὐτῶν
πνεύματι κρίσεως καὶ πνεύματι καύσεως. καὶ ἥξει,
καὶ ἔσται πᾶς τόπος τοῦ ὄρους Σιων καὶ πάντα τὰ
περικύκλῳ αὐτῆς σκιάσει νεφέλη ἡμέρας.

Μαρτυρεῖ καὶ τὸ κατὰ νόμον δὲ τῶν 'Ιουδαίων βάπτισμα.

[93] ϙ̅γ̅ ὅτι προκατηγγέλετο ἡ δευτέρα παρουσία--

[.1]   Μαλαχιας λέγει·

'Ιδοὺ ἔρχεται Κύριος παντοκράτωρ· καὶ τίς ὑπομενεῖ
ἡμέραν εἰσόδου αὐτοῦ; ἢ τίς ὑποστήσεται ἐν τῇ
ὀπτασίᾳ αὐτοῦ; διότι αὐτὸς εἰσπορεύσεται ὡς πῦρ
χωνευτηρίου καὶ καθιεῖται χωνεύων καὶ καθαρίζων.

[.2]   Καὶ πάλιν λέγει·

Προσάξω ὑμᾶς ἐν κρίσει καὶ ἔσομαι μάρτυς ταχὺς
ἐπὶ τοὺς φαρμακοὺς καὶ ἐπὶ τὰς μοιχαλίδας καὶ
ἐπὶ τοὺς ὀμνύοντας ἐπὶ τῷ ὀνόματι μου ἐπὶ ψεύδη.

[94] ϙ̅δ̅ ὅτι κρινεῖ τὴν οἰκουμένην καὶ αὐτῷ ἡ κρίσις δοθήσεται--

[.1]   Δαυιδ ἐν τῷ ϙ̅ε̅ ψαλμῷ λέγει·

Κρινεῖ Κύριος τὴν οἰκουμένην ἐν δικαιοσύνην.

[.2]   Καὶ Ιωηλ λέγει·

91.3 ελεησητε] ελεησηται 790. / εξαλειψατε] εξαλειψαται 790.
92   τω] om 790. / προκατηγγελετο] προκατηγγελλετο 28, 790.
92.1 υμων[1]] om 790. / ψυχων] καρδιων 790.
92.2 τραγωτερον] om 790. / καταλειφθεν] καταλαφθεν 28, καταληθθεν 790.
92.2 οτι[1]] om 790.
93   προκατηγγελετο] προκατηγγελλετο 28, 790.
93.1 εισπορευσεται] εισπορευεσεται 28.
93.2 επι[3]] εν 28. / επι[5]] εν 28.
94.1 Κυριος] om 790.

and smite and do not spare and have no mercy. Old and
young and women, nursing infants, destroy all; but do not
go near any upon whom is my mark.   [Ezek 9:3-6]

92 That baptism in Christ was foretold--

.1 Isaiah says,

Wash, become clean; remove your iniquities from your souls
before my eyes.   [Isa 1:16]

.2 And again, more plainly,

In that day, God will shine in counsel with glory over
the earth, to exalt and glorify the remnant of Israel
in Zion, and the remnant in Jerusalem, for all who are
appointed to live in Jerusalem will be called holy. For
the Lord will wash away the filth of the sons and daughters
of Zion, and he will purge out the blood of Jerusalem from
their midst by a wind which judges and a wind which burns.
And it will come, and a day-cloud will cover every place of
Mount Zion and all its surroundings.   [Isa 4:2-5]

(It also witnesses to the baptism according to the law of the
Jews.)

93 That the second coming is foretold--

.1 Malachi says,

Behold, the Lord almighty is coming; and who can endure the
day of his coming? Or who will withstand in his appearing?
For he will come as the fire of a furnace, and he will sit
judging and purifying.   [Mal 3:1-3]

.2 And again he says,

I will draw near to you in judgment, and I will be a swift
witness against the magicians and against the adulteresses
and against those who swear falsely in my name. [Mal 3:5]

94 That he would judge the inhabited world, and the judgment would
be given to him--

.1 In the 95th Psalm, David says,

The Lord will judge the inhabited world in righteousness.
                                                 [Ps 95:13]

.2 And Joel says,

a. Ἐγὼ ἥξω πάντα τὰ ἔθνη καὶ διακριθήσομαι πρὸς αὐτούς.

b. Καὶ ἔσται ἔμπροσθεν αὐτοῦ πῦρ ἀναλίσκον, καὶ τὰ
    ὀπίσω αὐτοῦ ἀναπτομένη φλόξ· καὶ τὰ ὀπίσω αὐτοῦ
    πεδίον ἀφανισμοῦ.

[.3] Καὶ πάλιν λέγει·
      Ἀπὸ προσώπου αὐτοῦ συντριβήσονται λαοί.

[.4] Καὶ πάλιν λέγει·
      Ὅτι κρίσις τῷ Κυρίῳ πρὸς τὸν λαὸν αὐτοῦ.

[.5] Καὶ Δανιηλ λέγει·
      Ἐθεώρουν ἐν ὁράματι τῆς νυκτὸς καὶ ἰδοὺ μετὰ τῶν
      νεφελῶν τοῦ οὐρανοῦ ὡς υἱὸς ἀνθρώπου ἐρχόμενος
      καὶ ἕως τοῦ παλαιοῦ τῶν ἡμερῶν ἔφθασε· καὶ αὐτῷ
      ἐδόθη ἡ ἀρχὴ καὶ ἡ τιμὴ καὶ ἡ βασιλεία, καὶ
      πάντες οἱ λαοί, φυλαί, γλῶσσαι δουλεύσουσιν αὐτῷ·
      ἡ ἐξουσία αὐτοῦ ἐξουσία αἰώνιος.

[.6] Καὶ Δαυιδ ἐν τῷ β̄ ψαλμῷ λέγει·
      Κύριος εἶπε πρός με· υἱός μου εἶ σύ,
      σήμερον γεγέννηκά σε·
      αἴτησαι παρ' ἐμοῦ, καὶ δώσω σοι ἔθνη τὴν κληρονομίαν
      σου
      καὶ τὴν κατάσχεσίν σου τὰ πέρατα τῆς γῆς.

[.7] Καὶ πάλιν ὁ αὐτὸς ἐν τῷ ō̄ε ψαλμῷ λέγει·
      Γῆ ἐφοβήθη καὶ ἡσύχασεν
      ἐν τῷ ἀναστῆναι εἰς κρίσιν τὸν θεὸν
      τοῦ σῶσαι τοὺς πραεῖς τῆς γῆς·
      ὅτι ἐνθύμιον ἀνθρώπου ἐξομολογήσεταί σοι.

[95] ō̄ε ὅτι ὁ ἥλιος καὶ ἡ σελήνη σκοτισθήσονται--

[.1] Ιωηλ λέγει·
      Δώσω τέρατα ἐν τῷ οὐρανῷ ἄνω
      καὶ ἐν τῇ γῇ κάτω,
      αἷμα καὶ πῦρ καὶ ἀτμίδα καπνοῦ·
      καὶ ὁ ἥλιος μεταστραφήσεται εἰς σκότος
      καὶ ἡ σελήνη εἰς αἷμα
      πρὶν ἢ ἐλθεῖν τὴν ἡμέραν Κυρίου τὴν μεγάλην καὶ
      ἐπιφανῆ·
      καὶ ἔσται πᾶς ὃς ἂν ἐπικαλέσηται τὸ ὄνομα Κυρίου
      σωθήσεται.

94.2b πεδιον] παιδιον 790, 28 illegible.
94.5   και¹] αι 790. / η¹] om 28.
94.6   αιτησαι] αιτησε 790.
94.7   ψαλμω] om 790. / εις...θεον] τον θεον εις κρισιν 28.
       σοι] om 28.

a. I will bring in all the nations and I will judge them.
[Joel 4:2]

b. And a consuming fire will be before him, and behind him a
burning flame; and behind it is a desolate plain.   [Joel 2:3]

.3 And again he says,

The people will be crushed by his presence.   [Joel 2:6]

.4 And again he says,

For the Lord has a judgment against his people.   [Mic 6:2]

.5 And Daniel says,

I saw in a night vision and behold one coming as a son of
man with the clouds of heaven, and he came up to the ancient
of days; and to him was given the rule and the honor and the
kingdom; and all the peoples, tribes, [and] languages will
serve him. His authority is an everlasting authority.
[Dan 7:13-14 (Th)]

.6 And in the 2d Psalm, David says,

The Lord said to me, You are my son,
today I have begotten you.
Ask from me, and I will give you the nations as your
inheritance
and the ends of the earth as your possession.   [Ps 2:7-8]

.7 And again in the 75th Psalm, the same one says,

The earth feared and was still
when God arose for judgment
to save the meek of the earth;
for the inward thought of man will praise you.   [Ps 75:9-11]

95 That the sun and moon would be darkened--

.1 Joel says,

I will show wonders in heaven above
and in the earth below,
blood and fire and vapor of smoke;
and the sun will be turned into darkness
and the moon into blood,
before the great and glorious day of the Lord comes.
And it will be that all who will call on the name of the
Lord will be saved.   [Joel 3:3-5; Acts 2:19]

[.2]   Καὶ πάλιν λέγει·

            Πάρεστιν ἡ ἡμέρα Κυρίου, ὅτι ἐγγὺς ἡμέρα σκότους
            καὶ γνόφου, ἡμέρα νεφέλης καὶ ὁμίχλης.

[.3]   Καὶ ὁ Ἐκκλησιαστὴς λέγει·

            Εὐφραίνου, νεανίσκε, ἐκ νεότητός σου,
            καὶ ἀπόστησον θυμὸν ἀπὸ καρδίας σου,
            καὶ μνήσθητι τοῦ κτίσαντός σε,
            ἕως οὗ μὴ ἔλθωσιν αἱ ἡμέραι τῆς κακίας σου,
            ἕως οὗ μὴ σκοτασθῇ ὁ ἥλιος
            καὶ ἡ σελήνη καὶ οἱ ἀστέρες,
            καὶ σκοτάσουσιν αἱ βλέπουσαι ἐν ταῖς ὀπαῖς.

[96]   ϙϛ ὅτι οἱ οὐρανοὶ εἰλίσονται--

[.1]   Ησαΐας λέγει·

            Καὶ εἰλισθήσεται ὡς βιβλίον ὁ οὐρανός, καὶ πάντα
            τὰ ἄστρα πεσεῖται ὡς φύλλα ἐξ ἀμπέλου καὶ ὡς
            πίπτει φύλλα ἀπὸ συκῆς.

[.2]   Καὶ ὁ Δαυιδ ἐν τῷ ρα ψαλμῷ λέγει·

            Κατ' ἀρχὰς σύ, Κύριε, τὴν γῆν ἐθεμελίωσας,
            καὶ ἔργα τῶν χειρῶν σού εἰσιν οἱ οὐρανοί·
            αὐτοὶ ἀπολοῦνται, σὺ δὲ διαμενεῖς,
            καὶ πάντες ὡς ἱμάτιον παλαιωθήσονται,
            καὶ ὡσεὶ περιβόλαιον ἑλίξεις αὐτούς, καὶ ἀλλαγή-
            σονται.

[.3]   Καὶ πάλιν Ησαΐας λέγει·

            Ὁ οὐρανὸς καὶ ἡ γῆ παρελεύσεται, οἱ δὲ λόγοι μου
            οὐ μὴ παρέλθωσιν.

[97]   ϙζ ὅτι πρὸ τῆς Χριστοῦ παρουσίας ἥξει ὁ Ἀντίχριστος--

            Δανιηλ λέγει·

            Ὀπίσω τούτων ἀναστήσεται βασιλεὺς ἕτερος, ὃς
            ὑπεροίσει κακοῖς πάντας τοὺς ἔμπροσθεν· καὶ
            λόγους πρὸ τὸν ὕψιστον λαλήσει.

[98]   ϙη ὅτι φονεύσει πολλούς--

            Δανιηλ λέγει·

            Ἐθεώρουν καὶ τὸ κέρας ἐκεῖνο ἐποίει πόλεμον μετὰ
            τῶν ἁγίων.

95.2 ημερα²] η ημερα 28.
96   ειλισονται] ειλιγησονται 28.
96.1 ειλισθησεται] ειλιγησσεται 28.
96.3 παρελευσεται] παρελευσονται 790.
97   υπεροισει] υπηρεισει 28, υπηρης' 790.

.2 And again he says,

> The day of the Lord is near, for a day of darkness and gloomi-
> ness is near, a day of cloud and mist.   [Joel 2:1-2]

.3 And Ecclesiastes says,

> Rejoice, young man, from your youth,
> and remove sorrow from your heart,
> and remember your creator,
> as long as the days of your evil have not come,
> as long as the sun is not darkened
> and the moon and the stars,
> and those who look out the windows will be darkened.
> [Eccl 11:9-12:3]

96 That the heavens would be rolled up--

.1 Isaiah says,

> And the heavens will be rolled up like a scroll, and all
> the stars will fall like leaves from a vine, and as leaves
> fall from a fig tree.   [Isa 34:4]

.2 And in the 101st Psalm, David says,

> In the beginning you, Lord, laid the foundation of the earth,
> and the heavens are the works of your hands;
> they will perish, but you will remain,
> and all will become old like a garment,
> and like a cloak you will fold them, and they will be
>   changed.   [Ps 101:26-27]

.3 And again Isaiah says,

> Heaven and earth will pass away,
> but my words will not pass away.   [Matt 24:35]

97 That before the appearing of Christ the Antichrist would come--

Daniel says,

> After those, another king will rise up, who will exceed all
> the former ones in evil; and he will speak words against the
> most high.   [Dan 7:24-25 (Th)]

98 That he would kill many--

Daniel says,

> I looked, and the horn made war with the saints.
> [Dan 7:21 (Th)]

[99]   Ϟϑ   ὅτι τότε καιρὸς θλίψεως--

       Δανιηλ λέγει·

       "Εσται τότε καιρὸς θλίψεως, θλῖψις οἷα οὐ γένονεν
       τότε ἐν ἀνθρώποις.

[100]   ρ̄   ὅτι μετ' αὐτὸν καὶ πῶς ὁ Χριστός--

  [.1]   Ζαχαριας λέγει·

       "Οψονται τὸν υἱὸν τοῦ ἀνθρώπου ἐρχόμενον ἐπὶ τῶν
       νεφελῶν· καὶ κόψονται φυλαὶ κατὰ φυλάς.

  [.2]   Καὶ Δαυιδ ἐν τῷ μ̄ϑ ψαλμῷ λέγει·

       Ὁ θεος ἡμῶν, καὶ οὐ παρασιωπήσεται·
       πῦρ ἐνώπιον αὐτοῦ καυθήσεται
       καὶ κύκλῳ αὐτοῦ καταιγὶς σφόδρα.

[101]   ρ̄α   ὅτι τὸ σημεῖον τοῦ Χριστοῦ φανερὸν ἔσται--

       Ησαϊας λέγει·

       Τότε φανήσεται τὸ σημεῖον τοῦ υἱοῦ τοῦ
       ἀνθρώπου, καὶ συναγάγων οὐ κατὰ τὴν δόξαν κρινεῖ
       οὐδὲ κατὰ τὴν λαλιὰν ἐλέγξει.

[102]   ρ̄β   ὅτι τῆς βασιλείας οὐκ ἔξει πέρας--

  [.1]   Δανιηλ λέγει·

       Ἡ βασιλεία αὐτοῦ οὐ διαφθαρήσεται, καὶ λαῷ ἑτέρῳ
       οὐχ ὑπολειφθήσεται.

  [.2]   Καὶ Δαυιδ ἐν τῷ μ̄δ ψαλμῷ λέγει·

       Ὁ θρόνος σου, ὁ θεός, εἰς τὸν αἰῶνα τοῦ αἰῶνος.

  [.3]   Καὶ πάλιν ὁ αὐτὸς ἐν τῷ ρ̄α λέγει·

       Σὺ δὲ ὁ αὐτὸς εἶ, καὶ τὰ ἔτη σου οὐκ ἐκλείψουσιν.

---

99   τοτε...θλιψεως] καιρος θλιψεως τοτε 790.
102.2   του αιωνος] om 790.
102.3   ο αυτος[1]] om 790.

99   That then the time of tribulation would come--

Daniel says,

Then will be a time of tribulation--tribulation such as has
not been before among men.   [Dan 12:1 (Th); Matt 24:21]

100 That somehow the Christ also would come with him--

.1   Zechariah says,

They will see the son of man coming on the clouds; and tribes
will mourn by tribes.   [Zech 12:10, 12; Dan 7:13 (LXX)]

.2   And in the 49th Psalm, David says,

He is our God, and he will not keep silence;
a fire will be kindled before him
and around him will be a great blast of wind.   [Ps 49:3]

101 That the sign of Christ would be plainly seen--

Isaiah says,

Then the sign of the son of man will appear,
and when he has gathered them together, he will not judge
according to appearance nor reprove according to report.
                                        [Matt 24:30; Isa 11:3]

102 That the kingdom would not have an end--

.1   Daniel says,

His kingdom will not be destroyed, and will not be left to
another people.   [Dan 2:44 (Th)]

.2   And in the 24th Psalm, David says,

Your throne, God, is for ever and ever.   [Ps 44:7]

.3   And again in the 101st Psalm, the same one says,

But you are the same, and your years will not fail.
                                              [Ps 101:28]

INDEX TO SCRIPTURAL CITATIONS IN THE TESTIMONY BOOK

GENESIS
1:26	2
49:9	71.3
49:10	5.1
49:11	37.2

NUMBERS
6:25	5.52
9:12	65
24:7	5.40
24:7	17b
24:8	26.2
24:9	71.4
24:17	5.41
24:17	17a

DEUTERONOMY
18:15-19	5.2
21:23	57.2
28:66	57.1
32:6	53.2

3 KINGDOMS
8:27	5.54

JOB
3:10-11	10
9:8	29
38:17	72.1
41:1-3	32.2

PSALMS
2:1-2	41.1
2:7-8	94.6
2:11	81.1
3:2-3	41.2
8:3	38
11:6	74.1
13:7	5.43
15:10	74.2
17:10	5.46
18:5	88.4
18:5-7	5.44
21:2	13a.2a
21:10-11	13a.2b
21:16	71.5
21:17	51.5
21:19	62

PSALMS (Cont.)
29:4	74.3
29:6	76.1
30:17	5.45
32:6	3.2
33:8	5.49
33:19	5.51
34:11-12	42.1
36:2	50
36:32	24.1
37:12	43.4
37:12	49.1
37:14	55.2
37:15	55.1
40:6-9	43.1
40:10	43.2
44:7	102.2
44:8	12.1
46:6	86.1
49:3	100.2
51:3-5	43.3
54:22-23	44.1
56:9	76.3
58:2-3	42.2
59:6	91.1
63:6-7	22
63:8	58.3
65:3	20
66:2	5.52
68:2-3	47.1
68:21	49.3
68:22	53.1
70:1-2	47.2
71:5	1.3
71:6	5.50
71:10-11	16.1
75:6	75
75:9-11	94.7
81:8	74.7
83:8	5.47
84:12	6.4
86:5	6.5
87:2	74.5
87:5	74.5
87:5	74.6
87:9	49.2
87:14	76.2
88:30	7.3

80

PSALMS (Cont.)		ISAIAH (Cont.)	
88:36-37	7.1	10:19	14.3
92:2	89.2	11:1-3	5.23b
95:13	94.1	11:3	101
96:6	5.53	11:10	5.27
97:3	5.53	14:9	72.2
101:26-27	96.2	19:1	25.1
101:28	102.3	19:21	25.2
106:16	72.3	25:8	34
106:20	4.4	25:9-10	36
108:1-2	44.2	26:19	85.2
108:25	56.1	27:11	81.2
109:1	89.3	28:16	13b.1b
109:3	1.1	30:10	84.2
111:10	21	33:16	15
111:10	24.2	33:16	66
117:26-27	5.48	33:17	5.24a
131:11	7.2	34:4	96.1
		35:3-4	33.1
PROVERBS		35:4-6	33.2
8:23-25	1.2	40:3	5.24b
8:27-30	3.1	40:9-10	5.24c
23:35	58.2	42:5-7	4.1
		45:14-15	5.28
ECCLESIASTES		45:14-15	6.9
11:9-12:3	95.3	49:7	48.2
		50:5-7	48.3
SONG OF SOLOMON		51:1	67
1:12	40	51:12-13	50
2:11-12	70	52:6-7	87.2
2:13-14	78	52:15	35b
3:1	79	53:1	35a
3:3	79	53:4-5	58.1
3:4	80	53:7	51.2
3:11	52.1	53:7	55.3
5:1	53.3	53:8	73.2
5:1	83	53:8-9	71.2
5:5	53.4	53:9	73.1
8:2	53.5	53:12	63
		57:1-2	71.1
ISAIAH		57:4	47.3a
1:16	92.1	60:6	16.2
2:2-3	5.22a	61:1	4.3
3:9-10	46.1	61:1	12.2
3:14	5.22b	61:1-2	87
4:2	5.23a	62:2	90.1
4:2-5	92.2	62:11	5.25
5:2	52.2	63:1-2	54
6:1	89.1	63:11	74.8
7:14	8	65:1	6.8
8:4	14.2	65:15-16	90.2
8:8-9	6.7	66:1	89.4
8:14	13b.1a	66:2	47.3b
8:16	91.2	66:7	11
9:5	14.1	66:14	5.26
9:6	7.4		

ZECHARIAH

2:14	5.18
3:1-2	32.1
3:9	13b.2
4:10	13b.2
6:12	5.19
8:2-3	5.20
9:9	5.18
9:9	37.1
9:11	85.3
11:12	45.1
11:13	45.2
12:10 (Heb)	64
12:10	100.1
12:12	100.1
14:6-7	59
14:6-7	60
14:16	88.1

MALACHI

1:14	5.21a
3:1	4.2
3:1	5.21b
3:1	37.3
3:1-3	93.1
3:5	39.1
3:5	93.2
3:20	5.21c
3:20	30

WISDOM OF SOLOMON

2:12	46.2
2:13	56.2b
2:14	46.2
2:18	56.2a
2:20	51.3
9:9	3.3

BARUCH

3:36-37	6.1
3:38	6.3

MATTHEW

1:23	8	"Isaiah"
2:11	16.2	"Isaiah"
2:15	26.1	"Joel"
24:21	99	"Daniel"
24:30	101	"Isaiah"
24:35	96.3	"Isaiah"
27:9-10	45.2	"Jeremiah"

JOHN

19:37	64	"Zechariah"

ACTS

2:19	95.1	"Joel"

ROMANS

9:33	13b.1a	"Isaiah"
9:33	13b.1b	"Isaiah"

GALATIANS

3:13	57.2	"Moses"

HEBREWS

13:20	74.8	"Isaiah"